PRESENT TRUTH LIFESTYLE

PRINCIPLES FOR VICTORIOUS LIVING

VOLUME II

MICHAEL SCANTLEBURY

Michael Scantlebury has taken author's prerogative in capitalizing certain words that are not usually capitalized according to standard grammatical practice. Also, please note that the name satan and related names are not capitalized as we choose not to acknowledge him, even to the point of disregarding standard grammatical practice.

Hebrew and Greek definitions are from James Strong, Strong's Exhaustive Concordance of the Bible (Peabody, MA: Hendrickson Publishers, n.d.).

Prayer Principles For Victorious Living - Volume II
ISBN: 978-1-7750222-0-6
ISBN: 978-1-7750222-1-3

Legal Deposit – Library and Archives of Canada, 2017

Published by Michael Scantlebury

Editorial Consultant: Anita Thompson – 604-521-6042

Cover design by: Dave Cropper of Cropper Media Limited – (868) 478-6618

BOOKS BY MICHAEL SCANTLEBURY

Victorious Prayer Principles – Volume I

Daniel: Apostle In Babylon

Esther: Present Truth Church

The Fortress Church

Called to be An Apostle – An Autobiography

Leaven Revealed

Five Pillars of The Apostolic

Apostolic Purity

Apostolic Reformation

Jesus Christ The Apostle and High Priest of Our Profession

Kingdom Advancing Prayer Volume I

Kingdom Advancing Prayer Volume II

Kingdom Advancing Prayer Volume III

Internal Reformation

God's Nature Expressed Through His Names

"I Will Build My Church." – Jesus Christ

Identifying and Defeating The Jezebel Spirit

PRESENT TRUTH LIFESTYLE

PRINCIPLES FOR
VICTORIOUS LIVING

VOLUME II

TABLE OF CONTENTS

ENDORSEMENTS

Michael Scantlebury has an obvious anointing. It particularly takes everything ranging from the Lord's and His Apostles' teachings to stories within the Old Testament to show us God's providence in supplying us with all that we need to live in the here and now in Kingdom victory. His keen insight that's evident in this book makes everything about the ancient writings of the Bible most current and practical, and can be applied to each day of our lives.

The information contained herein is well balanced with a spiritual maturity that keenly stems from wisdom and revelation in the knowledge of Christ. This is the anointing of an Apostle, and the truths that our brother shares will certainly cause you to excel in the Kingdom of God long before this life is over when later we enter the eternals. There's so much to experience today in this life, and Michael extracts so much from the Word of God to facilitate that. His insight of revelation and ability to interpret and articulate what his spirit receives from the Lord are powerful.

Michael Blume
Pastor & Bible Teacher
Breath of Life Church
Sidney, Manitoba

In the books" Present Truth Lifestyles Principles for Victorious Living Volumes 1 and 2" author Michael Scantlebury, a prolific writer, releases powerful truths about advancing the Kingdom of God in this time and season of the church. Kingdom techniques and spiritual technologies such a Kingdom advancing prayer intensifies the power and dedication of the Saints.

The initial purpose of the five-fold ministry is for the perfecting or maturing of the Saints, which leads to its next intention, which is the real work of the ministry of Jesus Christ, reconciling the world back to the Father. These books lend themselves as helps in the maturing of the Saints. They add insight and strategies that help in achieving exponential personal growth preparing one for the real work of the ministry. These are volumes of information and revelations needed in such a time as this, when maturity and focus are the needed key components that bring us an overcoming victory in this realm and advance the Kingdom of God.

Apostle Michael Scott Sr.
Lighthouse Covenant Ministries
Youngstown, Ohio USA

It is such a blessing to know Apostle Michael. His insights in the areas of prayer, spiritual warfare and the authority of the Saints are refreshing. If you are looking for superficial material that has cute bumper sticker quotes, Michael's books are not for you. But if you are going after the deep things of God, then run and get your hands on any of his many books. None of his writings will leave you feeling you've wasted your time reading. Go hungry and get fed. Go thirsty and get quenched.

I've enjoyed reading and re-reading Kingdom Advancing Prayers I, II and III. They have provided me with a deeper application and understanding of the Word (all of his prayers are Bible based). These current works are consistent with his past ones.

I believe that Apostle Michael is a prolific, gifted author that you will enjoy as much as I do.

Rev. Felix H. Anderson, D.Div.
President, Antioch International School of Ministry
Director, Healing Rooms of Bellingham

If any knows that the Church of Jesus Christ is in a furious battle with the unseen forces of darkness, Apostle Michael Scantlebury does. If any knows that prayer is the engine that advances the plan and agenda of God here in the earth, Apostle Michael Scantlebury does. If any knows that walking in divine revelation and understanding empowers the child of God by giving them supernatural advantage over the works of the flesh and the powers of darkness, Apostle Michael Scantlebury does.

It is written in Isaiah 33:6a **"Wisdom and knowledge** will be the stability of your times, **And** the strength of salvation;"

This excellently written book will give the reader guidance, encouragement, revelation, understanding, conviction and hope for living a victorious Christian life.

Apostle George Gadri
Founder: eEAGLE Ministries International
Durham, North Carolina

In every kingdom you need a strategy to navigate through the complexities of running the empire tactfully and successfully, and the wherewithal to overcome opposing kingdoms trying to overthrow it. In Apostle Michael Scantlebury's new book *Principles For Victorious Living (Volumes I & II),* strategic kingdom prayer tools have been given to us so that the Body of Christ can successfully navigate our King's agenda and extend and advance the Kingdom of God. In this present season prayer is a necessity for anyone who calls himself a man/woman of God.

Also in his book, Apostle Scantlebury will teach you how to become more effective in hearing the Father and teach you how to faithfully and obediently orchestrate His Kingdom objectives on planet earth through the power of prayer.

Apostle David M. Young Sr.
Senior Pastor – Prevailing Word World Outreach Center,
[http://prevailingwordwoc.org] New Castle PA
Coordinator – Kingdom Restoration Fellowship of Churches

Apostle Michael Scantlebury understands the dynamics of prayer. When reading this book, you'll know you are reading the words of a man who prays. Apostle Scantlebury quotes Mark 1:35, "Very early in the morning, while it was still dark, Jesus got up, left the house and went off to a solitary place, where he prayed." Jesus is our ultimate example and it is clear that Jesus took prayer very seriously.

Apostle Michael Scantlebury captures leading edge thoughts and revelation on advancing the Kingdom of God through prayer. He says, "New mindsets can be created at any stage of our lives to guide, instruct, shape and organize behaviour and action in our everyday life". It is time for old mindsets about prayer to be renewed and replaced with new perspectives and ideas on what prayer is all about. This book is filled with scripture coupled with strong revelation and perspectives on prayer.

If you want to know what is needed to be a Kingdom advancing prayer warrior, then this book is for you. Let us pray!

Pastor Marco Jacobs
El-Bethel Fellowship
Johannesburg, South Africa

Dr. Michael Scantlebury is an apostle of biblical literature, he has a gift to write and help people to discover their destiny, purpose and assignment in life. In order for them to pray into that assignment and see it birthed.

I am excited about his new book on, Principles For Victorious Living Volumes 1 and 2. He covers a vast number to topics, some of my favourites like "Apostolic Prayer Covering," which is vital for ministry. "Dismantling of Territories False gods." He also speaks about understanding the work of the Holy Spirit and reaping the benefits of possessing that understanding.

There is so much here to build up the Church to impact the community and nation, to release freedom and liberty in the Church and the world. Read it; pray it; and you will reap the benefits in your life and ministry.

Dr. Mark R. Van Gundy
Senior Pastor – Church of Destiny
www.churchofdestiny.org.uk

One of the missing dimensions in the church of Jesus Christ today is that of prayer. Some reasons could be that, people don't see the need for prayer, or the they don't have the time to pray. But prayer is a vital component to the church. It is its life; it is its sustenance.

Prayer became one of the main themes of the Early Church. As the church began to grow rapidly and the weight of the responsilbility of ministry increased, the Apostles realised that too much of their time was taken up with doing things other than what they were really called to do. So they told the church to choose seven men, who would assist them in the daily distribution of food to the Christian widows; so that they might give themselves continually to prayer and to the ministry of the word. Note which one had top priority-prayer.

The Apostles understood that prayer had to be the foundation of their lives and ministry and everything else flowed from it. In other words, without prayer, the ministry of the word may be good, but it would not be effective. Without prayer, they would not have the power to minister miracles and healing. Without prayer, their lives would become weak and unproductive and they would not have the ability to withstand persecution.

On one occasion Apostles Peter and John were arrested, jailed and brought before the Sanhedrin because they healed a man that was born paralysed. After questioning and threatening them, the Sanhedrin released them. This is what the Bible said happened next:

Acts 4:23–24
"On their release, Peter and John went back to their own people and reported all that the chief priests and

the elders had said to them. When they heard this, they raised their voices together in prayer to God."

Acts 4:31
"After they prayed, the place where they were meeting was shaken. And they were all filled with the Holy Spirit and spoke the word of God boldly."

They had good reason to complain, but instead, they prayed and asked God to give them boldness to declare His word and to do miracles. No wonder the Bible says that the prayer of a righteous person is powerful and effective. God is searching for those who will change situations; for His glory changes life's situations and circumstances through fervent, effective prayer.

This book, Present Truth Lifestyle, Principles For Victorious Living, will help you not just to develop an effective prayer life, but also give you different strategies in how to effectively pray. In addition to this, Apostle Dr. Michael Scantlebury will offer you from a very strong Biblical base, different aspects of prayer. Then he will show the results of effective, strategic prayer. May this book do more than challenge you; may it bring clarity and change your prayer life, so that you will be precise, effective and strategic every time you pray.

Apostle Stephen O. Holford
Senior Minister – New Dimensions Ministries
Barbados

INTRODUCTION

This book before you is the fifth in a series that have been published on prayer. The first three are titled Kingdom Advancing Prayer Volumes I-III. We decided to change the title and the cover design for this and the previous Volume.

Here is what Jesus said concerning the building of His Church:

"And I tell you that you are Peter, and on this rock I will build [*be building*] my church, and the gates of Hades will not overcome it." Matthew 16:18 [Parenthesis added]

These words of Jesus still echo through the tunnels of time, and now more than ever these words are relevant and very true. We have entered into the most significant time the Church and planet have ever experienced. The Church of Jesus Christ is now arising with awesome strength and power.

One of the keys to this amazing rise to greater functionality of the Church is the clear understanding of the dynamics of Prayer. The kind of prayer being referred to is the kind that reaches into the very core of the demonic stronghold and destroys demonic kings and princes and establishes the Kingdom of God and the Lord's Purpose. This is the kind of prayer that Jesus engaged in, to bring to pass the Will of His Father while He was upon planet earth. It is the kind of prayer that all the early Apostles and Saints functioned in!

Prayer has always been one of the most powerful tools the Church of Jesus Christ has in establishing the purposes of the Lord. The Apostle Paul, in writing to the church at Ephesus and by extension to us today, encourages us with the following words:

"Finally, *be strong in the Lord and in his mighty power.* 11 Put on *the full armour of God* so that you can take your stand against the devil's schemes. 12 For our struggle is not against flesh and blood, but against the rulers, against the authorities, against the powers of this dark world and against the spiritual forces of evil in the heavenly realms. 13 Therefore put on the full armour of God, so that when the day of evil comes, you may be able to stand your ground, and after you have done everything, to stand. 14 Stand firm then, with the belt of truth buckled around your waist, with the breastplate of righteousness in place, 15 and with your feet fitted with the readiness that comes from the gospel of peace. 16 In addition to all this, take up the shield of faith, with which you can extinguish all the flaming arrows of the evil one. 17 Take the helmet of salvation and the sword of the Spirit, which is the word of God. 18 And *pray in the Spirit on all occasions with all kinds of prayers and requests.* With this in mind, be alert and always keep on praying for all the saints." [Italics added Ephesians 6:10-18]

Prayer is as vital a part of our armour, as our waist being girded with truth, or as having on our breastplate of righteousness, or our feet being shod with the gospel, or having our shield of faith active, or our helmet of salvation or the sword of the Spirit.

Part of the technology that is being released into the Church as the Lord restores Apostles, is what we describe as Kingdom Advancing Prayer. This kind of prayer puts the

Kingdom of God first and foremost, it is above any personal need or agenda. However, as we engage in this type of prayer our lives are greatly enhanced and we also experience great victories in our personal lives. It is similar to the kind of prayer that [1]Elijah prayed, as the Lord used him to turn a whole nation around, and destroy the demonic influence that threatened to thwart the Lord's purpose. It is reflective of the prayer that [2]Jesus prayed as He prepared to bring to completion His Father's will and go to the cross.

The Church of Jesus Christ is stronger and much more determined and equipped than she has ever been; strong, aggressive, powerful, Spirit-Filled, Kingdom-Centred prayers are being lifted in every nation in the earth. We are seeing the emergence of Houses of Prayer all over the earth with prayer going up 24/7. Prayer is calling for the Bridegroom's return, and for the Bride to be made ready. Prayers that are storming the heavens and binding the "strong men", declaring and decreeing God's Kingdom rule in every jurisdiction. This is what we call Kingdom Advancing Prayer. This kind of prayer is released from the heart of Father God into the hearts of His people, as we seek for His Glory to cover the earth as the waters cover the sea. What a *Glorious Day* to be *alive* and to be in the *will and plan of Father God! Hallelujah*!

As I reflect on my walk and Christian life over the years, I want to thank the Lord for allowing the Holy Spirit to impress upon me the value, importance and need for prayer. I remember how He would waken me in the early hours of the day to go and pray. One of my favourite Scriptures that I practiced in those years and still do is Mark1:35, which simply say:

"Very early in the morning, while it was still dark,

---

[1] 1 Kings Chapter 18
[2] John Chapter 17

Jesus got up, left the house and went off to a solitary place, where he prayed."

I was also very impressed with what was hailed as Jesus' triumphant entry into Jerusalem and the events that took place that day. We read the account in Matthew 21:10-13.

"When Jesus entered Jerusalem, the whole city was stirred and asked, "Who is this?" 11 The crowds answered, "This is Jesus, the prophet from Nazareth in Galilee." 12 Jesus entered the temple area and drove out all who were buying and selling there. He overturned the tables of the moneychangers and the benches of those selling doves. 13 "It is written," he said to them, "`My house will be called a house of prayer,' but you are making it a `den of robbers.

Here we see Jesus establishing the importance of prayer in regard to the Plan and Purpose of God. He declared: *"My house will be called a house of prayer."* Just as it was true back then for the literal, physical Temple so it is absolutely true for the "Spiritual Temple" which is our bodies and by extension, the Church of Jesus Christ. Prayer is absolutely vital to any Kingdom advance and this cannot be overstated.

This is the fourth instalment in the series of books of a selection of teachings from our years of early Morning Prayer meetings, which we call "Kingdom Advancing Prayer", which is still ongoing here at Dominion-Life International Ministries [the ministry that my wife Sandra and I are privileged to have founded and lead]. It is my prayer that the chapters within this book would be a tool that can be used in furthering the cause of God's Kingdom in the earth, as well as providing strength and growth in your life. Be Blessed!

Chapter One

WHEN GOD IS SEEMINGLY LATE

What do you do when God seems to be late? When His turning up into your situation, regardless to what it is, does not appear to be as certain as you first thought; when His promises are not coming to pass according to your timetable! When according to your schedule He misses the date and stands you up; when He does not quite come through as expected. I do not mean when you have acted in your own flesh, or listened to 'Job's Counsellors' or when you have been deceived. I mean when you have a valid, bona-fide promise from Him...

For example like the case of Mary and Martha waiting for Jesus to show up for their sick brother Lazarus. They did everything in their power to contact Him in good time [John 11:2-3] but He never showed up on time to heal their brother from his sickness. By the time He did get there, the man had been buried for four days! As the KJV puts it 'He stanketh' [verse 39].

Another example can be cited in the case of Jeremiah who was waiting for God to destroy Jerusalem as He had prophesied all those years. Poor Jeremiah, in a fit of depression cried out, "LORD, you deceived me, and I was deceived; you overpowered me and prevailed. I am ridiculed all day long; everyone mocks me" [Jeremiah 20:7].

He probably felt a bit like Jonah whose dire prophecies never came to pass. He accused God saying, "Truly, you are to me like a deceitful brook, like waters that fail" [Jeremiah 15:18].

The question needing to be answered in such a case is—what shall I do? I seem to have done all that I could do and nothing seems to be working! Permit me the time to give you an answer. Firstly let me give a few pointers as to what not to do and then a few as to what you should do!

Don'ts
Don't Make Your Own God
After the Children of Israel left Egypt laden down with the wealth of their captors coming as a fulfillment to God's prophetic Word and His awesome dealings, they arrive in the Wilderness and Moses by the instruction of God, goes up the mountain to meet with Him! Aaron and the people were waiting for Moses to come down from the mountain with a word from God. God had already showed up and proved Himself time and time again to them, most recently the killing of the entire Egyptian army in the Red Sea! However, to them this time He seemed slack in sending Moses back with instructions to getting them to their Promised Land of blessings!

In the frustration of waiting, they made their own god in the form of a golden calf [Exodus 32:4]. In this they acted perversely [verse 7]. They made a god in their own image, [in the form they wanted to worship] from the gold they plundered from the Egyptians. They were quick to turn aside from the way God commanded them. They proved that they did not really know Him at all; all they were interested in were His acts and not His ways. So once again the essence of my first point is this—do not wander from God's ways.

Don't Make Your Own Offering
Saul was waiting on the hillside for Samuel to come and

make the sacrifice to God. He needed to adhere to right and godly order in the house; he was not qualified in God to offer up any sacrifice. When God's servant appeared late in coming, he bowed down to social pressure, and did the sacrifice himself [1 Samuel 13:9]. He did this twice [1 Samuel 15:21]. As a result, he was cursed, lost his kingdom and his anointing to lead. If God appears to be delayed in His coming, don't bow to social pressure. Do not enter into rebellion. Risk the riot—risk people rising up against you. David took the risk when he decided to pay the men for waiting with the bags, Jesus also took the risk when He told them He would not be crowned as king.

Don't Make Your Own Ministry

Abraham was "tricked" into trying his own fleshy method of fulfilling God's promise. His situation appeared hopeless. God had promised him children, but he was very old and weak. He appeared in the flesh to be unable to have children through his old and barren wife. So in the carnality of his flesh, he slept with Hagar [Genesis 16:3-4] and had thereby fathered an illegitimate son—Ishmael [Genesis 17:12]. When God seems late in answering, my advice to you is to wait for Him. Do not give in to your flesh.

When Abraham came to offer Isaac at the mountain God said, "Bring me your son, your only son Isaac". As far as God was concerned Ishmael did not even exist, he was not a son. At the end, all your works will be tested with fire, and your Ishmael's will not even exist anymore—they will be completely burned up. So please resist the temptation in bringing to pass God's Word to you in your own strength!

Don't Take Someone Else's Inheritance

Remember that infamous sibling rivalry and subsequent deception! Jacob knew in his heart that Esau was the father's favoured son [Genesis 25:28] and fought to steal his brother's birthright. He lied and deceived to get the father's blessing under the guise of being his brother [Genesis 27:32]. This is not the right way forward. If God appears late in blessing your circumstances, have patience. Do not lie and steal to get a blessing; it could turn out to be disadvantageous to you in the end.

Do's

Remember His Promises And His Good Works From The Past

Take the advice that Apostle Paul gave to his son in the Faith Timothy... Fight a good warfare according to the prophecies or promises given to you in times past [1 Timothy 1:18].

Remember what the Psalmist David said in Psalms 77:8-12 "Has his unfailing love vanished forever? Has his promise failed for all time? 9 Has God forgotten to be merciful? Has he in anger withheld his compassion?" Selah 10 Then I thought, "To this I will appeal: the years of the right hand of the Most High." 11 I will remember the deeds of the LORD; yes, I will remember your miracles of long ago. 12 I will meditate on all your works and consider all your mighty deeds."

Do Your Best Under The Given Circumstances

Joseph had some very great promises concerning his life and calling, yet he found himself in a pit, sold into slavery, thrown in jail and forgotten. The testimony regarding how Joseph carried himself in those years is clear, "Joseph became a successful man in the house of his Egyptian master" [Genesis 39:2-4]. Even in jail, Joseph worked hard, and God was with him—"and showed him steadfast love; he gave him favour in the sight of the chief jailer" [Genesis 39:21]. God prospered Joseph in every circumstance—even though they fell well short of the fulfilment of the promise. That was to come in the fullness of time! What God requires is that you work hard, and that you remain steadfast in your love, regardless.

Return To God Like Jeremiah: God offered Jeremiah the right hand of friendship. Though Jeremiah had accused Him of being deceitful, He offered a way back for the backslidden and depressed Prophet, "If you turn back, I will take you back, and you shall stand before me" [Jeremiah 15:19]. Repentance is the shortest path back into God's Will and good pleasure. He was able to say from then on, "The LORD is with me like a dread champion" [Jeremiah 20:11].

Seek First The Kingdom

Jesus said we are not to worry about our needs, nor indeed about anything in this world, we are to seek first the Kingdom of God and His Righteousness [Matthew 6:25-33]. We are to trust our Heavenly Father in all things and let Him take care of us and our needs. We are not to seek to "make" Him keep His promises, or try to force His hand [remember this—He Is A Covenant Keeping God!!!]. We are to trust quietly in Him, "In repentance and rest is your salvation; in quietness and trust is your strength" [Isaiah 30:15].

Jesus told the Disciples who were listening, "O you of little faith" why then do you worry? God is not sitting in Heaven biting his nails wondering how He is going to pay for you, or feed or clothe you. If you are stressed, or anxious then something is wrong—not with the Lord, but with you. We need to be reminded that God is in control. He does not exist within time as we understand it. He is eternal. A day is like a thousand years and a thousand years is like a day to Him [2 Peter 3:8].

In Closing, Please Remember This—God Is Not Slack!
2 Peter 3:9 states:
"God is not slack concerning his promise, as some men count slackness; but is longsuffering to us-ward." KJV

God is waiting for us, He is lining things up and very often it is our stubbornness, our slackness, our failure, our flesh, our lack of repentance that is holding things up.

Here are some encouraging passages of Scripture as you wait on the Lord:

Numbers 23:19
"God is not human, that he should lie, not a human being, that he should change his mind. Does he speak and then not act? Does he promise and not fulfill?"

"The LORD is faithful to all his promises and loving toward all he has made" [Psalm 145:13b]. The Lord's Character is to be trusted, He is in fact the only one to be trusted. If He does not come through on His word, no one can! God can not lie, He is not like a man. He is to be trusted. "God is not a man, that He should lie, nor a son of man, that He should change His mind. Does He speak and then not act? Does He promise and not fulfill?"

2 Corinthians 1:20
"For in him every one of God's promises is a "Yes." For this reason it is through him that we say the "Amen," to the glory of God."

Proverbs 3:5-6
"Trust in the LORD with all your heart and lean not on your own understanding; 6 in all your ways acknowledge him, and he will make your paths straight."

Hosea 6:2-3
"Let us acknowledge the LORD; let us press on to acknowledge him. As surely as the sun rises, he will appear; he will come to us like the winter rains, like the spring rains that water the earth."

Chapter Two

THE BENEFITS OF COMMITMENT

Jesus Christ calls for the Church to be a family of committed people. If He has called us to be this, then inevitably operating with such an attitude will bring certain benefits! But how does this work out in real life?

Commitment in the Church then means taking up responsibility which then restricts personal action and preference in favour of the Kingdom of God. This must involve a loss of independence and a corresponding gain of interdependence. One of the things that we must realize is this—our commitment to the Lord and the Church must result in us letting go of our personal fears or preferences in favour of obeying God's Word. As this is done there is what we call a symbiotic release where we are then free to receive the support of those He has joined us to. This in turn blesses us with an interdependence which achieves more than we could ever achieve on our own.

As we review the following passage, we must realize that Commitment may cost but once it is genuine then there will be no turning back.

> 1 Kings 19:19-21
> "And he left there, and found Elisha the son of Shaphat, and he was plowing; twelve pairs of oxen were before him, and he was with the twelfth. And

Elijah passed by him and threw his mantle on him. And he left the oxen and ran after Elijah, and said, Please, let me kiss my father and my mother, and I will follow you. And he said to him, Go back again, for what have I done to you? And he turned back from him, and took a yoke of oxen and killed them, and boiled their flesh with the instruments of the oxen, and gave it to the people, and they ate. And he arose and went after Elijah, and ministered to him."

As we see, Elisha rejected his status as a landowner and farmer to follow Elijah. In burning his plough and eating his oxen, Elisha demonstrated his commitment to Elijah, completely turning aside from his former life.

In stark contrast we have the following example recorded in the Book of Acts 5:1-14

"And a certain man named Ananias, with Sapphira his wife, sold a possession. And he kept back part of the price, his wife also knowing, and brought a certain part and laid it at the apostles' feet. But Peter said, Ananias, why has Satan filled your heart for you to lie to the Holy Spirit, and to keep back part of the price of the land? While it remained, was it not your own? And after it was sold, was it not in your own authority? Why have you conceived this thing in your heart? You have not lied to men, but to God. And hearing these words, Ananias fell down and expired. And great fear came on all those who heard these things. And the younger ones arose, wound him up, and carrying him out, they buried him. And it was about the space of three hours afterward, when his wife (not knowing what was done) came in. And Peter answered her, Tell me whether you sold the land for so much? And she said, Yes, for so much. Then Peter said to her, How is it that you have agreed together to tempt the Spirit of the Lord? Behold, the feet of those who have buried your husband are at the door and they will carry you out. Then at once she fell down at his feet and expired. And the younger ones found her dead, and, carrying her out, buried her beside her husband. And great fear came on all the church and on as many as heard these things. And many miracles and wonders were done among the people by the hands of the apostles; and they were all with one accord in Solomon's Porch. And of the rest no one dared to join himself to them, but the people magnified them; and more believing ones were added to the Lord, multitudes both of men and women..."

The preceding passage reveals that a sense of joining goes beyond superficial actions and relies instead on trusting the Lord God to do His part. Ananias and Sapphira did not die because they did not give enough, but because they gave out of a wrong motivation. They were concerned with looking generous before the Apostles while saving money for their own needs. This can happen with anything—not only money. These selfish desires prevented them from being fully joined to the Church. Acts also goes on to show that true joining is not an easy process. Despite the awful and very public consequences of Ananias and Sapphira's actions, the Church grew. Many people dared not join the Church when they saw the magnitude of what could happen, but nonetheless many were added by the Lord.

As an onlooker during this incident, you would probably judge the Apostles as unfair or unjust, but you would not see the other side of the story which is the fact that there was a prior agreement that all the proceeds from the sale of possessions were to be brought and laid at the Apostles' feet.

The Acts church is a model of the type of joining required by Christ—it is a call to live in the practice of the

Lord's design, not just the potential. For this to become a reality, commitment must come from every member of the group/community, with nothing held back. There can be no passengers, only crew members if there is to be a prophetic thrust.

In Hebrews 13:17 we read—"Yield to those leading you, and be submissive, for they watch for your souls, as those who must give account, that they may do it with joy and not with grief; for that is unprofitable for you."

Here we are reminded of the role of leadership in this whole issue of commitment. Those in authority will be called upon to give account for their flock. In order to do this it is essential that they know who the members of the flock are— those who are committed to the vision, leadership and direction of the church. If those they lead also accept this authority and submit to it, a relationship of genuine commitment benefits the group/community.

A crucial part of this is the corporate experience in the Holy Spirit. If we are fused together in the Holy Spirit we become an apostolic/prophetic people. In this type of relationship there is no room for a 'Lone Ranger' mentality as anyone with a self-serving attitude will never be fully committed to the group. Also, any joining without commitment distracts from what the Lord has given us to do. The parts of a body are interrelated— when someone stands on our toe, our mouth or hand will protest. If we trust a part of our body to fulfill an action and it cannot, the task we set out to do risks failure. Only when the parts of the body share the same experience can we expect to release and realize the benefits of commitment.

The Benefits of Commitment

As we are committed firstly to the Lord Jesus Christ and then to the Church He has placed us in we can Expect the following:

- A developmental care that goes beyond just meeting needs. The Church has always been seen as a place where people can receive help, love and care, yet pastoral care without commitment provides little more than what Government Agencies etc offer. When we commit ourselves to the leadership of a local church, the channel of His grace is opened and there is a flow which enables the leader to access God's power for a given situation. This is not just palliative care, but active development of the Word personally applied Galatians 6:6-10:

> "But let him who is taught in the Word share with the one teaching in all good things. Do not be deceived, God is not mocked. For whatever a man sows, that he also will reap. For he sowing to his flesh will reap corruption from the flesh. But he sowing to the Spirit will reap life everlasting from the Spirit. But we should not lose heart in well-doing, for in due season we shall reap, if we do not faint. So then as we have time, let us work good toward all, especially toward those of the household of faith."

Developments In Spiritual Growth

When there is greater expectation to hear, receive and be affected by the lives of those around us, there is great spiritual awakening. Luke 6:38 "give and it will be given to you"; the measure we 'give of ourselves' will be the measure we receive.

Ability to receive apostolic impartation, and the revelation that flows from this:

To fully receive apostolic impartation and revelation, we must be joined to and remain in pursuit of our relationship in our local Body of Believers. Remember that: "He who receives a prophet in the name of a prophet shall receive a prophet's reward. And he who receives a righteous man in the name of a righteous man shall receive a righteous man's reward." [Matthew 10:41]

The gaining of spiritual protection against erroneous doctrine and devices of satan:

Hebrews 13:7-9 admonishes us to: "Remember those leading you, who have spoken to you the Word of God, whose faith follow, considering the end of their conduct: Jesus Christ the same yesterday and today and forever. Do not be carried about with different and strange doctrines, for it is good for the heart to be established with grace, not with foods, in which those who have walked in them were not helped."

The sharing of blessing [and pain] through involvement in family life:
"Let love be without hypocrisy, shrinking from evil, cleaving to good; in brotherly love to one another, loving fervently, having led one another in honor. As to diligence, not slothful, fervent in spirit, serving the Lord; rejoicing in hope, patient in affliction, steadfastly continuing in prayer, distributing to the needs of the saints, pursuing hospitality. Bless those who persecute you; bless, and do not curse. Rejoice with rejoicing ones, and weep with weeping ones; minding the same thing toward one another, not minding high things, but yielding to the lowly. Do not be wise within yourselves. Repay no one evil for evil. Provide things honest in the sight of all men. If it is possible, as far as is in you, being in peace with all men not avenging yourselves, beloved, but giving place to wrath; for it is written, "Vengeance is Mine, I will repay, says the Lord." Therefore if your enemy hungers, feed him. If he thirsts, give him drink. For in so doing you shall heap coals of fire on his head. Do not be overcome by evil, but overcome evil with good." Romans 12:9-21

Remember that Family is God's order—He sets the solitary into a family! [Psalm 68:6]

There will be interdependence and not independence:

When we are truly committed then we gain a true sense of ownership of what the Lord is doing among the group/community. This leads to an increased sense of belonging, just as God intended. It is a motivation and forward thrust that turns away from independence. As a result we need to have a clear sense of the value of what the Lord God has given us. As such there can be no room for any 'loose canons' that ultimately damage the body with their need for independence. We should seek instead a commitment that will lead to genuine increase. When we are in the special place of belonging that the Lord has for us, we are then free to function as He intends. Only this committed joining will enable us to act as a truly apostolic/prophetic people.

Chapter Three
THE POWER OF PERCEPTION

In this life, most of our problems are due as a direct result of our perception or how we perceive things to be. In order to experience change we must first shift in our thinking. The Scripture alludes to this in Proverbs 23:7a "For as he thinks in his heart, so is he." Albert Einstein once said *"The significant problems we have cannot be solved at the same level of thinking we were at when we created them."* So in order for problems to be solved there must be a new level of perception thereby resulting in a new level of thinking.

The Definition of Perception is:

1. The act of perceiving or of receiving impressions by the senses; or that act or process of the mind which makes known an external object. In other words, the notice which the mind takes of external objects.

2. In philosophy, the faculty of perceiving; the faculty or peculiar part of man's constitution, by which he has knowledge through the medium or instrumentality of the bodily organs.

3. Notion, idea.

4. The state of being affected or capable of being affected by something external.

Perceive

1. To have knowledge or receive impressions of external objects through the medium or instrumentality of the senses or bodily organs; as, to perceive light or color; to perceive the cold of ice or the taste of honey.

2. To know; to understand; to observe.

3. Till we ourselves see it with our own eyes, and perceive it by our own understanding, we are in the dark.

4. To be affected by; to receive impressions from.

A classic Biblical example of the power of perception is found in the account of the Prophet Elisha and his servant In 2 Kings 6:15-20

"And when the servant of the man of God arose early and went out, there was an army, surrounding the city with horses and chariots. And his servant said to him, "Alas, my master! What shall we do?" 16 So he answered, "Do not fear, for those who are with us are more than those who are with them." 17 And Elisha prayed, and said, "LORD, I pray, open his eyes that he may see." Then the LORD opened the eyes of the young man, and he saw. And behold, the mountain was full of horses and chariots of fire all around Elisha. 18 So when the Syrians came down to him, Elisha prayed to the LORD, and said, "Strike this people, I pray, with blindness." And He struck them with blindness according to the word of Elisha. 19 Now Elisha said to them, "This is not the way, nor is this the city. Follow me, and I will bring you to the man whom you seek." But he led them to Samaria. 20 So it was, when they had come to Samaria, that Elisha said, "LORD, open the eyes of these men, that they may see." And the LORD opened their eyes, and they saw; and there they were, inside Samaria!" NKJV

In this passage, we have the account of two men with different visionary abilities. Elisha's servant saw the earthly dimension without seeing the heavenly dimension, while Elisha saw into both realms. Elisha was empowered by his seeing ability [perception] and very differently from his servant who could only respond with fear and alarm producing a negative influence on others. Elisha remained calm and in control by assuming his rightful position as God's representative in and for that moment. The difference with these two men and their ability to respond to life's presentation in that moment was their perception. Elisha could see the earthly and the spiritual realms while his servant saw only the earthly. Both men were sharing the same earthly dimensions, but each had their own unique spiritual positions based on their differing spiritual perceptions.

This poses these questions: What determines one's ability to see and perceive? What is your current ability to see and perceive that you are being limited by, or being empowered by? How can you ensure that you have a heavenly perspective on earthly situations or "real moments" as they occur?

Science reveals that we see with the mind while the eyes function simply as lenses. The mind perceives things in picture form and it does so very efficiently. The Scriptures reveal that understanding equals seeing or perception. Perception is therefore the visionary ability of the mind, which enables humans to respond to the realities that they see, perceive, and understand, whether physical or spiritual, earthly or heavenly.

The better or more accurate our spiritual perception, the more we are empowered to respond to life purposefully, meaningfully, and victoriously in relation to expressing the glory of God from the stewardship position given to us by God. Doctrine is part of spiritual perception and effects how accurately we see the heavenly reality amidst the earthly reality, and empowers us to respond appropriately. When we look at life and the events of the world around us, what are we seeing? What "perceptions" are influencing our conclusions, reactions or responses? Perception shapes reality! It produces a reality to us that we relate to whether our actions are right or wrong. Because we are seeing, and we are responding to what we are seeing with logic and sense, we assume we must be right. But heavenly perspective must be superimposed upon the earthly for accuracy to come forth. In essence we need to see what we believe!

People who have impaired vision will wear glasses, contact lenses or have laser surgery to bring correction to their vision. They are then able to respond to the dimensions of the natural realm better and with greater accuracy. People who have their spiritual vision impaired to any degree, need help to get their vision corrected. This is why Elisha prayed for God to open his servant's eyes. Otherwise his servant would have opposed him in his actions. The problem is that men have a tendency to assume that what they currently perceive in the natural is 20/20 vision whether it is indeed 20/20 vision or not, and that will be their reference point for any response or action until they choose to have their vision corrected.

Remember the account of Christopher Columbus who perceived the earth as being round in an age when most men perceived the earth to be flat as a table. People feared to venture out too far in their ships as they believed that they would fall off the edge of the earth. That seems ridiculous to us who live in an age/world where children grow up knowing that the earth is round. How many things have changed in the world as a result of Columbus' perceptions and convictions, and actions? Five hundred years after Columbus lived and proved his theory, we are reaping the benefits of the influence and impact of the accurate perceptions by a visionary named Columbus. I ask the question, "what difference does our perception make?" The answer is "every difference in the world" as perception with appropriate actions and discernment can change the very course of human existence as we know it. Big changes can come from a minority who are persistent and dedicated to their cause.

How significant are the ideas of a few among the majority that dismisses them as ridiculous and outrageous? Who ultimately benefits from the sacrifices made by that same few? All of humanity benefits! Yes, we are involved in changing the world forever, when we do the unthinkable against the traditional worldview of the majority who dismiss us as irrelevant, perhaps even ridiculous! Most people live their lives with the "if it isn't broke, don't fix it mentality" and are generally not receptive to the movers and shakers who think outside of the box. Perhaps they are even intimidated by the said visionaries. They are a source of contention at times as they are left to figure out and possibly oppose why and how we are willing and capable of abandoning the 'status quo', and examining over the long haul what are the benefits to mankind or to human experience. Columbus faced these backbenchers, and so will we. It all depends on how consistently we act in accordance with our perceptions.

Therefore in closing I would say to us—in order to have and maintain accurate perceptions in life as Born-Again Believers, our values and desire to please Father and do His Will must be at the very core of our value system. This must be the one thing that drives us in our journey to maturity whereby we improve our spiritual vision or perceptions of the heavenly realm—John 7:14-17 states:

"Now about the middle of the feast, Jesus went up into the temple and taught. (15) And the Jews marvelled, saying, How does this man know letters, not being taught? (16) Jesus answered them and said, My doctrine is not Mine, but His who sent Me. (17) If anyone desires to do His will, he shall know of the doctrine, whether it is of God, or I speak from Myself." NKJV

Chapter Four
VALUING THE GIFT OF THE HOLY SPIRIT

In this chapter I would like to encourage you to value the Gift of the Holy Spirit which has been freely given to us through Christ Jesus. This Gift is extremely precious and vital to our adoption as sons of God. It is made possible only through the sacrifice of Jesus Christ our Lord. It is good therefore for us to remember that the choices we make help to determine our level of cooperation and engagement with the Spirit of God, as well as the quality of relationship we share with the Father. The Word of God teaches that when we choose to draw near to God, He will draw near to us. This concept serves to remind us that the Spirit does not force Himself into our lives; He desires that we be actively involved in a process of thoughtful meditation, submission and engagement in His will.

Let us therefore be mindful of the urges of the Holy Spirit and be careful to obey His promptings.

A Reminder Of Who We Were
Ephesians 2:1-6
"As for you, you were dead in your transgressions and sins, 2 in which you used to live when you followed the ways of this world and of the ruler of the kingdom of the air, the spirit who is now at work in those who are disobedient. 3 All of us also lived among them at one time, gratifying the cravings of our sinful nature and following its desires and thoughts.

Like the rest, we were by nature objects of wrath. 4 But because of his great love for us, God, who is rich in mercy, 5 made us alive with Christ even when we were dead in transgressions-it is by grace you have been saved. 6 And God raised us up with Christ and seated us with him in the heavenly realms in Christ Jesus..."

These few verses remind us that at one time we were all dead in trespasses and sins. We were totally oblivious and unable to enjoy communion with the Father of all creation. Our sole purpose in life was to slavishly obey the dictates of the *spirit of disobedience*, falling prey to its attendant lust. But thanks be to God, Who did not leave us alone and helpless, but provided a way for us to escape this morass through the sacrifice of Jesus.

Who We Are In Christ
Ephesians 2:18-19
"For through him we both have access to the Father by one Spirit. 19 Consequently, you are no longer foreigners and aliens, but fellow citizens with God's people and members of God's household..."

Here we see when we accept the gift of Jesus Christ, it is His Spirit, [now resident in us], Who gives us access to the Father. We are no longer considered strangers and foreigners, but fellow citizens with the saints and members of the household of God. This is a far cry from the sorry condition we all shared prior to our encounter with Christ.

Galatians 4:4-6
"But when the proper time had fully come, God sent His Son, born of a woman, born subject to [the regulations of] the Law, 5To purchase the freedom of (to ransom, to redeem, to atone for) those who were subject to the Law, that we might be adopted and

have Sonship conferred upon us [and be recognized as God's sons]. [6]And because you [really] are [His] sons, God has sent the [Holy] Spirit of His Son into our hearts, crying, Abba (Father)! Father!" [Parenthesis added] AMP

Freedom In Christ

When we accept Jesus Christ as Lord, we also benefit from the package which He offers. Part of that package is the purchase of our Freedom. Remember that before we encountered Christ, we were blind, helpless and enslaved to sin. Verse 5 indicates that Christ purchased freedom for those who were subject to the Law. We are made free by the blood which He shed for us.

Hebrews 9:22 Says

"And according to the law almost all things are purified by means of blood, and without shedding of blood there is neither release from sin and its guilt nor the remission of the due and merited punishment for sins".

Sonship In Christ

Verses 5-6 further reveal that we have been given freedom so that we may be adopted and have Sonship conferred upon us. These verses are very comforting to us. God has sent the Holy Spirit to dwell within us. This Spirit cries Abba [Father]—signifying a new relationship with Him. We can call Him Father only because His Spirit now dwells in us thus making us 'sons', no longer strangers. With this in mind, we need to commit ourselves to a life that is worthy of those called 'sons of God'

Romans 8:9

"But you are not in the flesh but in the spirit, if indeed the Spirit of God dwells in you. Now if any-one does not have the Spirit of Christ, he is not His."

Chapter Five

Chapter Five

THE POWER OF IMPARTATION

As we continue to seek to be all that the Father has ordained for our lives, I would like for us to revisit what the Apostle Paul wrote in his letter to the Saints at Rome in Romans 1:11

"For I long to see you, that I may *impart* to you some spiritual gift, so that you may be *established*..." [Italics added]

The Definition Of Impartation

Impart comes from the Greek word "metadidomi", and in this context it means:

- The transfer of divine substance from God's realm to our earthly realm.

- It also means to give, grant or communicate; to bestow on another a share or portion of something; as, to impart a portion of provisions to the poor.

- It also means to grant; to give; to confer; as to impart honour or favour; to communicate the knowledge of something; to make known; to show by words or tokens.

The Bible declares that the end product/outcome of this kind of impartation is so that we become established!

Established is translated from both the Hebrew and Greek as the following:

- Rooted, firm, or fixed

- To set and fix firmly or unalterably

- To settle permanently

- To settle or fix

- To confirm; as to establish a person, society or corporation, in possessions or privileges.

Further meanings of the word are:
- To make firm

- To confirm

- To ratify what has been previously set or made

- To settle or fix what is wavering, doubtful or weak...

Two Things We Must Understand About Impartation For It To Truly Work
   1. Effective Release
   - Impartation gives authority to those ministering from an attitude of humility, to speak from the depths of their hearts to others.

   2. Effective Receiving
   - The person must be able to discern correctly and the heart of the individual must be right in order to achieve this accuracy without distortion.

   - There must be a removal of personal and ministry contaminations that pollute the heart.

   - Issues of ambition, pride, and cynicism, etc have no place in the individual, as it prevents the word from taking root in the heart. Remember the Parable of Sower where Jesus talked about seed being planted into the good soil of the heart in order for it to thrive.

- There must be a proper honouring of the apostolic grace [this apostolic grace is, the impartation that comes from the Lord upon the one carrying the Apostolic Call and Anointing...]—please understand that honour is not an outward act where one appears to confer esteem on something, but to be personally convicted that God sent this apostolic gift into your life.

Luke 8:18—"*Therefore consider carefully how you listen. Whoever has will be given more; whoever does not have, even what he thinks he has will be taken from him.*" [Italicized]

Chapter Six

FAITHFULNESS!

In this chapter I offer you a teaching from Br. David Reid, one of our leaders, here at Dominion-Life International Ministries.

I would like for us to focus on a very important word which appears in Scripture. This word helps to define a major attribute resident in our God; consequently, it must also define who we are. This word is "Faithful". The original word used in Scripture is the word 'Pistos'. When used as a verbal adjective, it conveys the meaning of "to be trusted and reliable"

Trusted and Reliable; that speaks to one of the Qualities of our God!

Our God is Faithful
1 Corinthians 1:4-13
"I thank my God always concerning you for the grace of God which was given to you by Christ Jesus, 5 that you were enriched in everything by Him in all utterance and all knowledge, 6 even as the testimony of Christ was confirmed in you, 7 so that you come short in no gift, eagerly waiting for the revelation of our Lord Jesus Christ, 8 who will also confirm you to the end, *that you may be* blameless in the day of our Lord Jesus Christ. 9 *God is faithful*, by whom you were

called into the fellowship of His Son, Jesus Christ our Lord. [10] Now I plead with you, brethren, by the name of our Lord Jesus Christ, that you all speak the same thing, and *that* there be no divisions among you, but *that* you be perfectly joined together in the same mind and in the same judgment. [11] For it has been declared to me concerning you, my brethren, by those of Chloe's *household,* that there are contentions among you. [12] Now I say this, that each of you says, "I am of Paul," or "I am of Apollos," or "I am of Cephas," or "I am of Christ." [13] Is Christ divided? Was Paul crucified for you? Or were you baptized in the name of Paul?" [Italics Added] KJV

Verses 4-6 remind us of the fact that the church at Corinth was indeed rich in the distribution and demonstration of spiritual gifts. The following verses of this passage however, reveal the troubling situation which Paul was attempting to address. There was division among the members of the church. When Paul wrote in response to this problem, he thought it necessary to remind the Saints of the faithfulness of God. This divine characteristic brings assurance of the reliability and trustworthiness of God. It seems as though Paul chose to inject the antidote of 'faithfulness' in an attempt to overcome the negative effects brought about by division within the body.

Father and Son Are One

Paul further proceeded to admonish the Saints to be of the same mind and judgment because Jesus Christ is not divided, nor is there any contention between Him and the Father. The same qualities and characteristics found in the Father is also resident in the Son.

Colossians 2:9-10

"For in Him dwells all the fullness of the Godhead bodily; [10] and you are complete in Him, who is the head of all principality and power."

We Share His DNA

Since there exist such cohesion between Father and Son, we too are required to be faithful stewards, continuously working towards unity of mind and thought.

Ephesians 1:1
"Paul, an apostle of Jesus Christ by the will of God, To the saints who are in Ephesus, and *faithful in Christ Jesus:*" [Italics added]

Colossians 1:1-2
"Paul, an apostle of Jesus Christ by the will of God, and Timothy our brother, ² To the saints and *faithful brethren in Christ who are* in Colossi: Grace to you and peace from God our Father and the Lord Jesus Christ." [Italics Added]

Since our new identity is found in Jesus Christ, we too must exhibit Christ like qualities.

The Word of God also teaches that it is the *faithful* among the brethren who can be trusted and relied upon to preserve and teach the purity of the Word of God.

2 Timothy 2:1-2
"You therefore, my son, be strong in the grace that is in Christ Jesus. ² And the things that you have heard from me among many witnesses, commit these to *faithful* men who will be able to teach others also." [Italics Added]

Let me take this opportunity to remind you that our faithful Father has given unto us all things that pertain unto life and godliness. He is carefully orchestrating the events of life to bring us all to an expected end. As faithful stewards therefore, be encouraged, commit to eliminating divisions wherever they may appear among us and continue to put your faith, trust and reliance on Him.

Chapter Seven

MINISTRY OF RECONCILIATION!

L et me take this opportunity once again to offer you another teaching by Br. David Reid, one of our leaders. It is my earnest prayer that we all experience growth and maturity as we continue the process of preparing ourselves as the Bride [the Body] of Christ. Remember it is His desire to reconcile the world to Himself and to us have been given the word of reconciliation. We must therefore remain strong and committed to the task at hand.

Psalm 8
"O LORD, our Lord, how excellent (majestic and glorious) is Your name in all the earth! You have set Your glory on [or above] the heavens. ²Out of the mouths of babes and unweaned infants You have established strength because of Your foes, that You might silence the enemy and the avenger. ³When I view and consider Your heavens, the work of Your fingers, the moon and the stars, which You have ordained and established, ⁴What is man that You are mindful of him, and the son of [earthborn] man that You care for him? ⁵Yet You have made him but a little lower than God [or heavenly beings], and You have crowned him with glory and honour. ⁶You made him to have dominion over the works of Your hands; You have put all things under his feet: ⁷All

sheep and oxen, yes, and the beasts of the field, [8]The birds of the air, and the fish of the sea, and whatever passes along the paths of the seas. [9]O Lord, our Lord, how excellent (majestic and glorious) is Your name in all the earth!" AMP

His Handiwork Reveals His Glory:

Having made careful observation of the handiwork of God, this psalmist exclaims "how excellent (or glorious) is Your name in all the earth"! We can all see the awesome glory of God revealed in His creation. The moon and the stars as they adorn the heavens, speak of the vastness of His glory. Yet this great God looked favourably upon man, the object of His creation and has bestowed a greater glory and honour upon him. Verse 5

Man is Crowned With Honour:

The divine favour bestowed upon man actually means that God has chosen to crown him (man) with glory and honour. As a result of this, man has been given the wisdom and authority to exercise dominion over God's handiwork, and to have all things subject to him—Verse 6. This view is consistent with God's original plan for man which is captured in Genesis Chapter 1:

Genesis 1:26-28.

"God said, Let Us [Father, Son, and Holy Spirit] make mankind in Our image, after Our likeness, and let them have complete authority over the fish of the sea, the birds of the air, the [tame] beasts, and over all of the earth, and over everything that creeps upon the earth. 27So God created man in His own image, in the image and likeness of God He created him; male and female He created them. 28And God blessed them and said to them, Be fruitful, multiply, and fill the earth, and subdue it [using all its vast resources in the service of God and man]; and have dominion over the fish of the sea, the birds of the air, and over every living creature that moves upon the earth."

The Effects of Sin

When sin came into the earth, the relationship between God and man was compromised. However, the charge to be fruitful and multiply, as well as to have dominion over all of God's creation was not removed. What changed was man's relationship with God. This severed relationship significantly affected the manner in which man was to execute his divine mandate. Sin brought death [Romans 6:23], blindness, selfishness, wickedness and the like into the administration of man. I am certain that we do not have to look very far to see the devastating consequences of sin. It may be advisable to start with our own lives, then look at wider local, regional and global issues. Some of the issues which are quite apparent are; poverty, sickness, wars, pollution, global warming, etc. Man by his many acts of disobedience has brought chaos into the order which existed within all of God's creation. We can now better understand why all of creation is waiting and groaning for the manifestation of the sons of God. See Jeremiah 12:4;11 and Romans 8:19-23. There is undoubtedly a dire need for the reconciliation of man.

Ministry of Reconciliation
2 Corinthians 5:19-21
"It was God [personally present] in Christ, reconciling and restoring the world to favour with Himself, not counting up and holding against [men] their trespasses [but cancelling them], and committing to us the message of reconciliation (of the restoration to favour). 20So we are Christ's ambassadors, God making His appeal as it were through us. We [as Christ's personal representatives] beg you for His sake to lay hold of

the divine favour [now offered you] and be reconciled to God. [21]For our sake He made Christ [virtually] to be sin Who knew no sin, so that in and through Him we might become [endued with, viewed as being in, and examples of] the righteousness of God [what we ought to be, approved and acceptable and in right relationship with Him, by His goodness]." [Parenthesis Added]

The Apostle Paul in this passage reminds us that one of the purposes of Christ coming to earth was to reconcile the world to God and to commit to us [His Church], this ministry of reconciliation. Since we are all members of this powerful, glorious, undeniable entity called the Church, we too must also equip ourselves as Ambassadors of Christ conveying this message of reconciliation to the world.

We must all learn to focus on the truth from God's Word which has the ability to build faith and endurance in us. We must also ignore the false messages of the world which has the ability to produce fear and doubt. Contrary to popular opinion, this world cannot exist without the presence and prayers of the Saints. Let us therefore, continue with greater determination to engage in the process of reconciling man back to God.

Chapter Eight
SOME DYNAMICS OF PRAYER AND INCENSE

" **A**nd when He had taken the book, the four living creatures and the twenty-four elders fell down before the Lamb, each one having harps and golden vials full of incense, which are the prayers of the saints." Revelation 5:8

"And when He opened the seventh seal, there was silence in Heaven for about half an hour. And I saw the seven angels who stood before God, and seven trumpets were given to them. And another angel came and stood at the altar, having a golden censer. And many incenses were given to him, so that he should offer it with the prayers of all saints on the golden altar before the throne. And the smoke of the incense which came with the prayers of the saints, ascended up before God from the angel's hand. And the angel took the censer and filled it with fire from the altar, and cast it into the earth. And voices and thunderings and lightnings and an earthquake occurred." Revelation 8:1-5

These Scripture Verses reveal an awesome and powerful truth regarding our prayers that ascend to Heaven. As we explore this dynamic called prayer, we also want to look at the other component that was used to effect powerful movements in the earth. Also remember that prayer is a direct communication between the two realms and is much more than simply words uttered upon the earth.

In Revelation 5:8 the prayer of the Saints are identified as incense and in Chapter 8:4 we see both the incense from Heaven and the incense identified as the prayer of the Saints ascending before God from the angel's hand. There is also a subsequent response as a result of the prayer. Fire is tossed into the earth from the altar and there are physical manifestations of noises, thunderings, lightnings and earthquakes.

In light of this, it will be beneficial for us to explore the significance of incense [prayers] in the Word of God. Incense was used throughout the Old Testament as a means of communicating with God. One of the first places we see this occurring is under Moses in Exodus 30:1-8.

"And you shall make an altar to burn incense upon. You shall make it of acacia-wood. A cubit shall be its length, and a cubit its breadth. It shall be square. And two cubits shall be the height of it, its horns from itself. And you shall overlay it with pure gold, its top, and its sides all around, and its horns. And you shall make to it a crown of gold all around. And you shall make two golden rings to it under the crown of it, by the two corners of it, upon the two sides of it you shall make it. And they shall be housings for the staves to bear it with. And you shall make the staves of acacia-wood and overlay them with gold. And you shall put it before the veil that is by the ark of the testimony, in front of the mercy-seat that is beside the testimony, where I will meet with you. And Aaron shall burn sweet incense on it every morning; when he dresses the lamps he shall burn it. And when Aaron lights the lamps at evening, he shall burn it, a perpetual incense before Jehovah throughout your generations."

Here we see that Moses was required to make an Altar of Incense which was to be overlaid with pure gold and placed before the veil that was by the Ark of the Testimony... in the place "where I will meet with you". This represented a meeting place with God and it was to burn sweet incense—declared to be "perpetual incense" to be burnt throughout your generations.

As we continue, let us briefly look at what constituted the sweet incense [prayers] that were to be perpetually offered up to God.

> "And Jehovah said to Moses, Take to yourself sweet spices, stacte, and onycha, and galbanum; sweet spices with pure frankincense, a part of each one. And you shall make it a perfume, an incense according to the art of the perfumer, salted, pure and holy. And you shall beat some of it very small, and put it before the testimony in the tabernacle of the congregation, where I will meet with you. It shall be most holy to you. And the perfume which you shall make, you shall not make any for yourselves according to the way it is made. It shall be holy to you for Jehovah. Whoever shall make any like that, to smell of it, shall even be cut off from his people." Exodus 30:34-38

Some important points about incense as it relates to prayer:

Incense was balanced in its makeup [verse 34], made up of equal parts of different sweet spices and pure frankincense. This shows us that we ought to be balanced not only in our approach to prayer, but also in our prayer of itself. Jesus spoke about vain repetitions and empty prayers to the Pharisees.

Incense was mixed together with deliberate skill according to the art of the perfumer [verse 35]. Therefore, we should approach prayer very seriously and pray that way. Jesus gave His early Apostles the art of praying in Matthew Chapter 6.

The incense that was brought before the Ark of the Testimony had to be beaten "very small or fine" which represents the excellence of the meeting place. The incense was reserved only for God. It was holy to you for Jehovah [verse 37].

It was forbidden to use the sweet-smelling incense for personal use. Death was stipulated as the required punishment. These prayers that the incense represents could not be selfishly manipulated for personal gain and ambition. It was unto the Lord. [James 4:3 "You ask and receive not, because you ask amiss, that you may spend it upon your lusts."]

Another dynamic of this incense could be found when Aaron made atonement for himself; Scripture declares that as he did this, his life was protected. In like manner we need to offer sweet incense beaten fine [quality prayers] for ourselves before the Presence of the Lord and cause His Great Fire to fall from heaven upon our lives; Leviticus 16:11-13

"And Aaron shall bring the young bull of the sin offering which is for himself, and shall atone for himself and for his house, and shall kill the young bull of the sin offering which is for himself. And he shall take a censer full of coals of fire from off the altar before Jehovah, and his hands full of fragrant perfumes beaten small, and bring it within the veil. And he shall put the incense on the fire before Jehovah. And the cloud of the incense shall cover the mercy-seat that is on the Testimony. And he shall not die."

King David understood this principle which he demonstrated in Psalm 141:

"A Psalm of David. O Jehovah, I cry to You; make haste to me, give ear to my voice when I cry to You. Let my prayer be set forth before You as incense, and the lifting up of my hands as the evening sacrifice. Set a watch, O Jehovah, before my mouth; keep the door of my lips. Let not my heart turn aside to any evil thing, to practice wicked works with men who work iniquity; and let me not eat of their delicacies. Let the righteous strike me; it shall be a kindness; and let him correct me, it is oil on my head, let not my head refuse it; for still my prayer also shall be against their wickedness. When their judges are overthrown in stony places, they shall hear my words; for they are sweet. Our bones are scattered at the grave's mouth, as when one cuts and splits wood on the earth. But my eyes are on You, O Lord Jehovah; in You I take refuge, do not leave my soul naked. Keep me from the traps which they have laid for me, and the snares of the workers of evil. Let the wicked fall into their own nets together, while I escape."

As we continue in our study of Prayer/Incense, there is another side to our offering of Incense/Prayer before the Lord that I want you to briefly look at—the "negative" side.

In Numbers Chapter 16 we read of the issue that came up that caused the Lord to move against Korah, Dathan, Abiram and On in the camp and destroy them. The whole point of this incident is the way in which the proper offering of incense, ties in with a deep understanding of divine order and spiritual authority in the ranks of Israel.

Korah, Dathan, Abiram and On offended the Lord in a number of ways:

- They revolted against the vision of the company in standing against Moses and Aaron and insisting on a spiritual parity with them. In verse 3 they declared "And they gathered themselves against Moses and against Aaron, and said to them, You take too much upon you, since all the congregation are holy, every one of them, and Jehovah is among them. Why then do you lift yourselves up above the congregation of Jehovah?"

- They declared that the move of God was inaccurate and in essence God did not know what He was doing. Listen to them in verses 13-14

    "And Moses sent to call Dathan and Abiram, the sons of Eliab. And they said, We will not come up. Is it a small thing that you have brought us up out of a land that flows with milk and honey (there are speaking about Egypt), to kill us in the wilderness, but must you also seize dominion over us? Besides, you have not brought us into a land that flows with milk and honey, nor given us inheritance in fields and vineyards. Will you put out the eyes of these men? We will not come up."

- They called Egypt the land of milk and honey and complained that the manifestation of the new vision [arriving in the Promised Land; a Land overflowing with milk and honey] had been delayed and probably will never be seen. But deep inside, their complaint was a true revolt. It was a revolt against the authority of Moses and Aaron ["but must you also seize dominion over us?"] to lead the people. Rebellion had crept into their hearts and they refused to come up when summoned.

- Their attitude of rebellion and arrogance was contagious; and as such they also polluted the hearts of 250 other men of the tribes who willingly followed them in their error. Behind all this of course, operating unseen and unrecognised, is the enemy satan who attempts to bring the stain of impurity into the incense/prayer offerings of the people—[verses 16-17 inform us of this]—"And Moses said to Korah, Stand before Jehovah, you and all your company, you and they, and Aaron, tomorrow. And every man take his fire-pan and put incense in them, and let every man bring his fire-pan before Jehovah, two hundred and fifty fire-pans, you also, and Aaron, each with his fire-pan."

In Leviticus 10:1-7 we read of another powerful example of this from a slightly different perspective but the end result was the same.

"And Nadab and Abihu, the sons of Aaron, each took his censer and put fire in it, and put incense on it, and offered strange fire before Jehovah, which He had not commanded them. And there went out fire from Jehovah and devoured them, and they died before Jehovah. Then Moses said to Aaron, It is that which Jehovah spoke, saying, I will be sanctified in them that come near me, and before all the people I will be glorified. And Aaron held his peace. And Moses called Mishael and Elzaphan, the sons of Uzziel, the uncle of Aaron, and said to them, Come near, carry your brothers from before the sanctuary out of the camp. And they came near and carried them in their coats out of the camp, as Moses had said. And Moses said to Aaron and to Eleazar and Ithamar his sons, Do not uncover your heads nor tear your clothes, lest you die, and lest He be angry on all the people. But let your brothers, the whole of Israel, mourn the burning which Jehovah has kindled. And you shall not go out of the door of the tabernacle of the congregation, lest you die. For the anointing oil of Jehovah is on you. And they did according to the word of Moses."

Here we see Nadab and Abihu, the sons of Aaron offered strange incense [prayer] and fire before the Lord and they are instantly killed by fire. Nadab and Abihu were the oldest of Aaron's four sons and as such they were ranked right after their father, the High Priest. You could be sure that they were not ignorant of all the complex regulations of the priesthood in which they served with their father. They were the custodians of the purity of the service of the Tabernacle, and their task was to assist in directing the people towards the Lord and maintaining the forward momentum of the march through the wilderness towards the Land of Promise.

Not only did they have the knowledge of the demands of the work but they also had revelation of the nature and person of God Himself. In Exodus Chapter 24 Nadab and Abihu along with Moses, Aaron and the seventy Elders of Israel were summoned by name to come up to the mountain to meet with God. They see a dimension of the Lord's Glory [verses 9-10] shining "like the very heavens in its clarity". They are "the anointed Priests" [Numbers 3:3] and they have an intimate knowledge of the power and preciousness of the Lord's anointing. These men did not offer strange fire by mistake. They undoubtedly had been performing in the service of the Lord for quite some time before that awful error entered their lives. God's reaction was swift and decisive. There are simple yet profound messages for us in this incident as we discern how we should operate in the Lord's service and thereby continuously evaluate ourselves according to our increasing knowledge of the demands of the service of the Lord.

The regulation that was given to Moses was that all incense offered before the Lord had to be offered on coals taken from the fire that was to be kept perpetually burning on the altar of incense. No fire could be kindled outside the context of that burning, for it would be strange or profane fire. The principles from this passage of Scripture that we can apply to our lives are clear and awesome. When we come before the Lord as a corporate body and stand in our position to prevail for the purposes of God for our lives here and across the earth, we are ministering in a priestly capacity before Him. No strange or profane fire must be offered before the Lord. The sin of the brothers was the sin of familiarity with the routine, which they had done so often before in the conduct of their priestly duties, that they had lost the sense of the importance and "specialness" of each occasion.

Saints, please understand this—we must never, because of familiarity, come to the place of prayer with a sense of routine. We must not be careless and thus be inaccurate in the fire of our heart, speaking to God with a sense of bore-dom, inattention, blind to the fact that in our every encounter with the Presence of God, our Mighty Divine Sovereign [Abba Father] stirs Himself afresh to move in the earth in response to our cry, as effectively and as powerfully as He did the very first time we called unto Him. In the mind of God repetition does not dull the insistent importance of our prevailing prayer. Each time must be as filled with a sense of the preciousness as did the first time. Before God there must be no "strange fire".

In other words the integrity, clarity and wholeness of our Incense/Prayer offering indicate our level of regard for the Person of God when we come into His Presence. When coming before God in prayer we must:

- Not be in a state of inner rebellion against the vision of the Moses/Aaron's order of the house.

- Not be looking backward into "Egypt" but expectantly forward to the promise that is unfolding before us.

- Be offering prayer that is consistent with the present vision of the house [local church] that you are a part of. There must be no strange fire!

Chapter Nine
PURITY OF HEART!

As we continue to walk towards maturity and the ultimate fulfillment of our destiny, we need to obtain a clear sight of our Father as He leads us. This clarity of sight is made possible when we maintain purity of heart. I believe that this is a season when God is emphasizing His requirement for purity of heart among believers. This condition is necessary because, without it we will fail to recognize Him every time. We may become busy with many activities, but fail to see the unveiling of the plan and purpose of God in our lives.

> Psalm 24:3-6
> "Who may ascend the hill of the LORD? Who may stand in his holy place? 4 He who has clean hands and a pure heart, who does not lift up his soul to an idol or swear by what is false. 5 He will receive blessing from the LORD and vindication from God his Saviour. 6 Such is the generation of those who seek him, who seek your face, O God of Jacob. Selah"

This is a Psalm of David who we know was a man after God's own heart. When we study the life of this patriarch we will discover that he placed much emphasis on the condition of his heart. His writings are replete with cries of reflection and repentance so that he may possess a pure heart before God.

From his own experience this psalmist declares that the man who has clean hands and a pure heart will be permitted to ascend to 'the hill of the Lord'. 'The hill of the Lord' in this context can be described as the place of blessings, victory and elevated sight. Verse 5 states that this man shall receive blessing and righteousness from the God of his salvation.

A Pure Heart is maintained by Accurate Response to the Word of the Lord!

If we should fall into sin, God has made provision for us all, but we must respond to Him in the prescribed manner. It is futile for us to seek to cover up or hide our sin from Him. An example of the correct response is seen in the life of David after Nathan the Prophet revealed that his sin with Bathsheba was ever present before the Lord.

Psalm 51:1-12
"Have mercy on me, O God, according to your unfailing love; according to your great compassion blot out my transgressions. 2 Wash away all my iniquity and cleanse me from my sin. 3 For I know my transgressions, and my sin is always before me. 4 Against you, you only, have I sinned and done what is evil in your sight, so that you are proved right when you speak and justified when you judge. 5 Surely I was sinful at birth, sinful from the time my mother conceived me. 6 Surely you desire truth in the inner parts ; you teach me wisdom in the inmost place. 7 Cleanse me with hyssop, and I will be clean; wash me, and I will be whiter than snow. 8 Let me hear joy and gladness; let the bones you have crushed rejoice. 9 Hide your face from my sins and blot out all my iniquity. 10 Create in me a pure heart, O God, and renew a steadfast spirit within me. 11 Do not cast me from your presence or take your Holy

Spirit from me. [12] Restore to me the joy of your salvation and grant me a willing spirit, to sustain me."

Even though God sent the Prophet to confront David in his sin, yet it is his response that holds the key to the success of this patriarch. He did not try to silence the Voice of the Lord, nor did he attempt to make excuses for his sinful deeds. This king bore his broken and penitent heart before the Lord, crying out for forgiveness. In his confession David also declared something that we should all take note of. In Verse 6 he declared that our God desires truth in the inner parts. This speaks of a divine requirement for purity of heart.

Purity of Heart—A Divine Standard

Wilful disobedience proceeds from a corrupt heart. To resolve this situation, David also prayed in Verse 10 for God to create a pure heart and renew a steadfast spirit within him. Let us always remember therefore, that our God requires purity of heart for all Saints. There are no exceptions. Without this, we will fail to see or recognize the many ways in which He is working through the varied situations of our lives. Consequently, we will find ourselves fighting against the will and purpose of God, without understanding, having been disqualified to participate in it.

The Pure in Heart Will See God
Matthew 5:8
"Blessed are the pure in heart, For they shall see God."

Finally, let me simply introduce one other thought relevant to this issue. Jesus Christ Himself declared that it is the Pure in Heart that will see God. Those whose hearts are pure will occupy the enviable place of blessings, favour and sight. I have chosen in this letter, to place an emphasis on the aspect of sight. The pure in heart shall see God! This must not be interpreted as merely a futuristic sight of God.

We must understand that this refers to an elevated level of sight in the present as well as future. It is the pure in heart therefore, who shall possess the ability to discern the mind of the Father in the midst of life. This is the heritage of all Saints of the Most High God.

Chapter Ten

THE ACHILLES' HEEL FACTOR

I n this chapter permit me the grace to use some Greek Mythology to portray a necessary truth as we continue to unveil principles for a victorious life.

An Achilles' heel is a deadly weakness in spite of overall strength, that can actually or potentially lead to downfall. While the mythological origin refers to a physical vulnerability, metaphorical references to other attributes or qualities that can lead to downfall are common. In Greek mythology, when Achilles was a baby, it was foretold that he would die in battle from an arrow in the foot. Naturally, his mother Thetis did not want Achilles to die. So she took Achilles to the River Styx, which was supposed to offer powers of invincibility, and dipped his body into the water. But as Thetis held Achilles by the heel, his heel was not washed over by the water of the magical river. Achilles grew up to be a man of war who survived many great battles. As the story goes, there was a Trojan war and Achilles went to war and was killed by the Trojan prince Paris, Helen's kidnapper, who, with Aphrodite's help, shot an arrow into his only weak spot—his heel. Yet Achilles is remembered as one of the greatest fighters who ever lived.

As Born-Again Believers we must understand that we are involved in a war. This war is being waged on several fronts, and we need to always be on guard and to be aware of the devices of our enemy the devil. One of the areas that we need to be very mindful of is being "over confident" in our standing in the plan and purpose of the Lord. If the enemy can cause us to become "over confident", [Hebrews 10:35] then we would step into realms and battles that we are not graced for. We would also run the risk of running ahead of God, missing His perfect timing and hence being defeated.

The Apostle Paul in 1 Corinthians 10:1-11 gives us a powerful example of areas that we need to be careful to guard lest we are destroyed.

"Moreover, brethren, I do not want you to be unaware that all our fathers were under the cloud, all passed through the sea, all were baptized into Moses in the cloud and in the sea, all ate the same spiritual food, and all drank the same spiritual drink. For they drank of that spiritual Rock that followed them, and that Rock was Christ. But with most of them God was not well pleased, for their bodies were scattered in the wilderness. Now these things became our examples, to the intent that we should not lust after evil things as they also lusted. And do not become idolaters as were some of them. As it is written, "The people sat down to eat and drink, and rose up to play." Nor let us commit sexual immorality, as some of them did, and in one day twenty-three thousand fell; nor let us tempt Christ, as some of them also tempted, and were destroyed by serpents; nor complain, as some of them also complained, and were destroyed by the destroyer. Now all these things happened to them as examples, and they were written for our admonition, on whom the ends of the ages have come." 1 Corinthians 10:1-11

Paul then puts his whole admonition into perspective in verse 12:

"Therefore let him who thinks he stands take heed lest he fall." NKJV

"So, if you think you are standing firm, be careful that you don't fall!"

For those of us who drive, there is something called "a blind spot"—that is the area in our rear-view and wing or side mirror that we cannot see. One's inability to see in that "blind spot" has been the cause of many serious, and sometimes fatal, accidents. Hence, due care and attention must be given in that area, especially when we have to change lanes or direction.

In like manner, in our journey of life we also have a responsibility to keep alert at all times. We should not be passive in the driving force that leads us through life. When God gives us direction, we must not lose our focus on Him, or be led astray by satan, who attempts to sneak into our blind spot. A collision with him could mean a total change in our direction, with devastating consequences.

So as we continue in our faith-filled, victorious prayer life, let us be mindful to check/protect our blind spots or any known area of weakness that the enemy could exploit.

Chapter Eleven

REPLACING DOUBT WITH REAL FAITH

It may be correct to say that there are times when circumstances of life press us to be consumed by thoughts of worry and doubt. It is also correct to say that it is impossible to become excited about something when there is doubt in our minds. Let us take another look at what the Scripture says about doubt and faith so that we can be assured of victory in every aspect of our walk with Christ.

> James 1:5-8
> "If any of you lacks wisdom, let him ask of God, who gives to all liberally and without reproach, and it will be given to him. 6 But let him ask in faith, with no doubting, for he who doubts is like a wave of the sea driven and tossed by the wind. 7 For let not that man supposes that he will receive anything from the Lord; 8 he is a double-minded man, unstable in all his ways." NKJV

The principle to observe here is; 'faith activates the hand of God while doubt causes our path to become unstable and robs us of divine blessings.'

There can be no excitement in instability and depravity, but those who are full of faith will rejoice in the provisions of the Lord. Apostle James reminds us that there is an abundant supply available to meet our needs. The promise is that God will give liberally to all who ask in faith. This is a season for all saints to upgrade the level of faith that resides within.

There is a very good example of faith at work in the account of the woman with the issue of blood:

Mark 5:25-34

"Now a certain woman had a flow of blood for twelve years, [26] and had suffered many things fro many physicians. She had spent all that she had and was no better, but rather grew worse. [27] When she heard about Jesus, she came behind Him in the crowd and touched His garment. [28] For she said, "If only I may touch His clothes, I shall be made well." [29] Immediately the fountain of her blood was dried up, and she felt in her body that she was healed of the affliction. [30] And Jesus, immediately knowing in Himself that power had gone out of Him, turned around in the crowd and said, "Who touched My clothes?" [31] But His disciples said to Him, "You see the multitude thronging You, and You say, 'Who touched Me?'" [32] And He looked around to see her who had done this thing. [33] But the woman, fearing and trembling, knowing what had happened to her, came and fell down before Him and told Him the whole truth. [34] And He said to her, "Daughter, your faith has made you well. Go in peace, and be healed of your affliction."

Remove Doubt and Excuses

This woman could have held on to many excuses based on the harsh reality of her life. These excuses would have created doubt and thereby deprived her of obtaining the healing which she pursued for many years.

She Suffered Long

She could have focused on the variety of things which she had suffered at the hands of many physicians over the past 12 years. We must bear in mind that the practice of physicians in that day was not as refined nor were their approaches to medicine based on proven scientific observation as it is today.

She Would Have Been Considered Unclean
Her condition would have rendered her unclean. She could have used that as an excuse not to pursue her healing among the crowd which followed Jesus.

She Would Have Been Weak
She had opportunity to consider the physical weakness of her own body brought about by this prolong period of illness. This condition might have caused many to doubt their ability to press through that crowd in an attempt to obtain healing.

She Grew Worse Over Time
In spite of her persistent efforts and financial losses, she grew worse over time.

Possess Real Faith
Not withstanding the overwhelming negative circumstances of her life, this woman chose to exercise real faith in Christ Jesus to provide her healing. Her faith was so real; she did not require a face to face encounter with Him. In her mind she resolved, 'If I could only touch the hem of His garment, I know I will be made whole.' This faith was the key that unlocked the healing virtues of Christ in her life.

Real Faith Releases Divine Virtue
I believe that there were many needs present among the crowd of people surrounding Jesus at that moment. There were those who simply desired to be present to see the miracles which He did. There were those who were pressing to engage His attention, as well as those who protected Him from the press of the crowd. In the midst of all this activity, the one thing that caught the attention of

Christ was that one slight touch of real faith. This slight touch of faith was enough to release divine healing for this woman.

Real Faith Commands the Attention of Christ

The response of Jesus assures us that He is hardwired to the frequency of 'real faith.' Every time we act in faith, He is alerted and responds favourably to our prayers. This woman did not have the privilege of conversing face to face with Jesus. She simply struggled to touch His garment from behind, yet Jesus knew that virtue had left Him. This quality of faith caused Jesus to turn around, [temporarily suspending His forward advance] to enquire and to declare a complete blessing on the woman.

Let us therefore work on eliminating doubt and worry from within us and replace them with real active faith. There is an abundant supply available for those who act in faith. Remember that without faith it is impossible to please Him [God]!

CHAPTER TWELVE

OVERCOMING WORRY AND RESTORING HOPE

In this chapter I will like us all to reflect on an aspect of Christian living which captured the attention of the Saints of the Early Church. This has to do with maintaining a healthy perspective in life through careful consideration of things around us. One of the original words which is translated 'to consider', is the word 'katanoeo'. Some of the strains of meaning of this word are:

- To perceive clearly.

- To understand fully.

- To consider closely.

- To fix ones thoughts on.

- To take a good hard look at.

Examples of the use of this word can be seen in the following Passages of Scripture:

Consider The Ravens And Lilies

Luke 12:24; 27-31

"Consider the ravens: They do not sow or reap, they have no storeroom or barn; yet God feeds them. And how much more valuable you are than birds! 25Who of you by worrying can add a single hour to his life?

26Since you cannot do this very little thing, why do you worry about the rest? 27"Consider how the lilies grow. They do not labour or spin. Yet I tell you, not even Solomon in all his splendour was dressed like one of these. 28If that is how God clothes the grass of the field, which is here today, and tomorrow is thrown into the fire, how much more will he clothe you, O you of little faith! 29And do not set your heart on what you will eat or drink; do not worry about it. 30For the pagan world runs after all such things, and your Father knows that you need them. 31But seek his kingdom, and these things will be given to you as well."

These were the words of Jesus Christ when He taught an innumerable multitude of people who were gathered to hear Him. In these few verses Jesus gives the key to living life with the right perspective. His teaching was certainly contrary to the prevailing mentality of the day. His admonition to a people overcome by worry over earthly things was to seek first the things which pertain to God's Kingdom and all other things will be given to them.

The systems of this world are all designed to press us towards selfishness, competition and worry. These concepts reinforce the condition that denies faith in us. Through these systems, we are taught that for us to succeed, others must fail. We are also conditioned to believe that the best way to reach to the top is by pulling others down.

Jesus teaches that success through faith can be our portion when we take time to carefully consider the manner in which the Father takes care of the ravens and the lilies [things around us]. Now, I am certain that Jesus Christ came, suffered, died and rose again for the benefit of all mankind. This great sacrifice was not made for the benefit of the ravens or the lilies. His sacrifice was to provide a secure way for all of mankind to be brought into a renewed relationship with the Father. Jesus' reasoning was, since we are of greater value than the lilies and ravens, how much more will our Father provide for and take care of us.

> Consider The Apostle And High Priest Of Our Faith
> Hebrews 3:1-6
> "Therefore, holy brothers, you who share in a heavenly calling, consider Jesus, the apostle and high priest of our confession, 2who was faithful to him who appointed him, just as Moses also was faithful in all God's house. ³For Jesus has been counted worthy of more glory than Moses—as much more glory as the builder of a house has more honour than the house itself. ⁴(For every house is built by someone, but the builder of all things is God.) ⁵ Now Moses was faithful in all God's house as a servant, to testify to the things that were to be spoken later, ⁶but Christ is faithful over God's house as a son. And we are his house if indeed we hold fast our confidence and our boasting in our hope." ESV

In this passage, the author reminds us that Jesus Christ is worthy of our complete devotion. We should take time to consider Him less we become entrapped by the systems of this world. This entrapment is designed to dull the cutting edge of our commitment and obedience to Him. Let us therefore consider Him who is worthy of more glory than Moses. In these verses we are admonished to take a good hard look at the Apostle and High Priest of our confession. By this we will be able to hold fast to the confidence, boasting and hope which we have in Jesus Christ.

Chapter Thirteen
WHAT IS THAT YOU HAVE IN YOUR HAND?

We often use the excuse that we don't know what we are called to do in the Kingdom. We sometimes say, "I can't preach, I can't sing, I don't know enough of the Bible to share with someone else". Consequently, we miss many opportunities that God allows to cross our paths each day. We are waiting for our local assembly to organize some program or event so that we can share our Kingdom beliefs. As a part of the whole Body of Christ every joint, cell, and organ need to contribute to cause the Body of Christ to function effectively.

Ephesians 4:16 states:
"...from whom the whole body, joined and knit together by what every joint supplies, according to the effective working by which every part does its share, causes growth of the body for the edifying of itself in love.

I would like to share just a few examples of people in the Bible who used their awkward circumstances and not use excuses to prevent them from sharing or making what ever they had available to be used as a blessing to others.

Little Maid: 2 Kings 5:1-27
"Now Naaman, commander of the army of the king of Syria, was a great and honourable man in the eyes

of his master, because by him the LORD had given victory to Syria. He was also a mighty man of valour, but a leper. 2 And the Syrians had gone out on raids, and had brought back captive a young girl from the land of Israel. She waited on Naaman's wife. 3 Then she said to her mistress, "If only my master were with the prophet who is in Samaria! For he would heal him of his leprosy." 4 And Naaman went in and told his master, saying, "Thus and thus said the girl who is from the land of Israel." 5 Then the king of Syria said, "Go now, and I will send a letter to the king of Israel." So he departed and took with him ten talents of silver, six thousand shekels of gold, and ten changes of clothing. 6 Then he brought the letter to the king of Israel, which said Now be advised, when this letter comes to you, that I have sent Naaman my servant to you, that you may heal him of his leprosy." NKJV

This little girl although held captive did not withhold the fact that she knew a Prophet who could bring healing to her master. She served her mistress so well in spite of her captivity that her mistress did not hesitate to act on the little maid's advice. Naaman eventually got his complete healing through a little girl's testimony; this little girl, who was not even given a name in the Bible. This miracle also became known throughout the region, that the God of the Israelites was a Mighty Healer.

The Widow At Zerephath: 1 Kings 17:8-15
"Then the Lord said to Elijah, 9 "Go and live in the village of Zarephath, near the city of Sidon. I have instructed a widow there to feed you." 10 So he went to Zarephath. As he arrived at the gates of the village, he saw a widow gathering sticks, and he asked her, "Would you please bring me a little water in a cup?"

11 As she was going to get it, he called to her, "Bring me a bite of bread, too." 12 But she said, "I swear by the Lord your God that I don't have a single piece of bread in the house. And I have only a handful of flour left in the jar and a little cooking oil in the bottom of the jug. I was just gathering a few sticks to cook this last meal, and then my son and I will die." 13 But Elijah said to her, "Don't be afraid! Go ahead and do just what you've said, but make a little bread for me first. Then use what's left to prepare a meal for yourself and your son. 14 For this is what the Lord, the God of Israel, says: There will always be flour and olive oil left in your containers until the time when the Lord sends rain and the crops grow again!" 15 So she did as Elijah said, and she and Elijah and her son continued to eat for many days. 16 There was always enough flour and olive oil left in the containers, just as the Lord had promised through Elijah." NKJV

Here again is a woman, a widow having just enough food left to feed herself and her son in a time of famine. She was getting prepared to eat her last meal with her son and then wait to die with him. Most likely she would have watched her son die first and then she may have died soon after. What a gruesome thought. This widow's willingness to share her last meal with the Prophet, released a divine supply, which was enough to preserve her life and that of her son. Our willingness to give to God what we may think insignificant may also be the beginning of our own breakthrough.

The Little Boy With Five Loaves And Two Fishes: John 6:1-14
"After this, Jesus crossed over to the far side of the Sea of Galilee, also known as the Sea of Tiberias. 2 A

huge crowd kept following him wherever he went, because they saw his miraculous signs as he healed the sick. 3 Then Jesus climbed a hill and sat down with his disciples around him. 4 (It was nearly time for the Jewish Passover celebration.) 5 Jesus soon saw a huge crowd of people coming to look for him. Turning to Philip, he asked, "Where can we buy bread to feed all these people?" 6 He was testing Philip, for he already knew what he was going to do. 7 Philip replied, "Even if we worked for months, we wouldn't have enough money to feed them!" 8 Then Andrew, Simon Peter's brother, spoke up. 9 "There's a young boy here with five barley loaves and two fish. But what good is that with this huge crowd?" 10 "Tell everyone to sit down," Jesus said. So they all sat down on the grassy slopes. (The men alone numbered about 5,000.) 11 Then Jesus took the loaves, gave thanks to God, and distributed them to the people. Afterward he did the same with the fish. And they all ate as much as they wanted. 12 After everyone was full, Jesus told his disciples, "Now gather the leftovers, so that nothing is wasted." 13 So they picked up the pieces and filled twelve baskets with scraps left by the people who had eaten from the five barley loaves. 14 When the people saw him do this miraculous sign, they exclaimed, "Surely, he is the Prophet we have been expecting!" 15 When Jesus saw that they were ready to force him to be their king, he slipped away into the hills by himself." NKJV

We are not expected to give what we don't have, but we are expected to give what we do have! When the disciples could round up only five loaves and two fish, the Lord didn't tell them to be ashamed of themselves. But neither did He tell them to forget His command to feed the huge crowd even though they could come up with only five small loaves and two small fish. This would hardly be enough to feed one person, let alone "make a dent" in the hunger of the multitude. The disciples were expected to give what they had to meet the need. The Lord took on Himself the responsibility for multiplying the resources.

Our responsibility is to give what we have to Him--not more, but not less! The little we have can meet the greatest need when it is given to Christ and then multiplied by Him. Think of it! More than 5,000 [possibly as many as 12,000, counting women and children] were fed with only five loaves of bread and two fish that a little boy gave to the disciples. The little boy could have said, "I am so lucky that my mother was wise to give me these five loaves and two fishes. I'll keep it to myself; these people should have been prepared. It is not enough to share. Actually I wished I had ten loaves and four fishes, I am so hungry". No, this little boy shared the little he had and a mighty miracle was displayed.

In Exodus 4:1 when God asked Moses to help to deliver the Israelites from Egypt, this is what Moses did: But Moses protested again, "What if they won't believe me or listen to me? What if they say, The Lord never appeared to you?" NKJV

This was God's response: Exodus 4:2 "Then the Lord asked him, "What is that in your hand?" "A shepherd's staff," Moses replied." NKJV

With that staff, Moses defeated the magicians of Egypt, stripped Pharaoh of his power, humiliated Egypt's gods and brought Israel out from slavery to freedom on the edge of the Promised Land.

How many spiritually hungry people who need Christ are on your campuses, your neighbourhoods or in your places of employment? Did you say several thousand? What do you have to give? Did you say you have only a small stammering testimony for Christ? Give what you have! Your small but faithful testimony and your quiet consistent life can affect the entire campus or corporation for the Lord in an almost unbelievable way! Like Moses, God is asking, "what do you have in your hand?" Let us all offer what ever we have to give.

Chapter Fourteen

FINANCIAL BLESSINGS: PRINCIPLES FOR INCREASE

T his particular letter was sent out to our members and our mailing list one December, hence the reference following: In this season where there is such a tendency to spend, spend and then spend some more I would like to cover some aspects of Financial Blessings; and also to give you a few principles for increase:

God Is The Source

The first principle that we need to completely understand and flow in is that God is the source of everything in our lives. Here are a few Scriptures noteworthy of exploring:

Philippians 4:19 says:

"And my God shall supply all your need according to His riches in glory by Christ Jesus."

Proverbs 8:20-21 adds:

"I traverse the way of righteousness, In the midst of the paths of justice, 21 That I may cause those who love me to inherit wealth, That I may fill their treasuries.

And 2 Corinthians 9:8 says:

"And God is able to make all grace abound toward you, that you, always having all sufficiency in all things, may have an abundance for every good work."

Giving Is Essential For Increase

The second principle is that of giving.

Luke 6:38, a key verse, says:

"Give, and it will be given to you: good measure, pressed down, shaken together, and running over will be put into your bosom. For with the same measure that you use, it will be measured back to you."

According to Deuteronomy 14:23 one purpose of tithing was to teach the people of Israel to honour and to fear the Lord and to put Him first in their lives...

"And you shall eat before the LORD your God, in the place where He chooses to make His name abide, the tithe of your grain and your new wine and your oil, of the firstborn of your herds and your flocks, that you may learn to fear the LORD your God always."

Proverbs 3:9-10 reads:

"Honour the LORD with your possessions, And with the first-fruits of all your increase; 10 So your barns will be filled with plenty, And your vats will overflow with new wine."

Save—The Bible Supports Saving

The third financial principle concerns saving money—i.e. setting something aside for a "rainy day".

Proverbs 21:20 says:

"There is desirable treasure, And oil in the dwelling of the wise, But a foolish man squanders it."

And Proverbs 22:3 emphasizes:

"A prudent man foresees evil and hides himself."

Keep Out Of *Unnecessary* Debt

The fourth principle is to keep out of unnecessary debt and thus avoid the debt trap. Borrowing for a house or car is one thing but taking on financial obligations one can't keep—i.e. buying beyond your ability to pay—is another.

Psalm 37:21 says:
"The wicked borrows and does not repay, But the righteous shows mercy and gives."

The minute a person goes into debt, he loses a portion of his freedom. As Proverbs 22:7 says:
"The rich rules over the poor, And the borrower is servant to the lender."

Too many people think you can buy now and pay later. That isn't true. I've found that "easy credit" now makes people "bound" later. Usually a person pays more for the use of borrowed money than he gets in interest for saving it.

Contentment—A Powerful Secret!
The fifth principle is being content with what one has.

Hebrews 13:5 puts it succinctly:
"Let your conduct be without covetousness; be content with such things as you have. For He Himself has said, "I will never leave you nor forsake you."

1 Timothy 6:6-8
"Now godliness with contentment is great gain. 7 For we brought nothing into this world, and it is certain we can carry nothing out. 8 And having food and clothing, with these we shall be content."

Hard Work Or Work Hard
The sixth principle is that of hard work. The Scriptures spell it out in Proverbs 14:23:
"In all labour there is profit, But idle chatter leads only to poverty."

Proverbs 28:19
"He who tills his land will have plenty of bread, But he who follows frivolity will have poverty enough!".

Proverbs 18:9
"He who is slothful in his work Is a brother to him who is a great destroyer."

Proverbs 21:25
"The desire of the lazy man kills him, For his hands refuse to labour."

It is important to work. "In the beginning God created" [Genesis 1:1]. Even God is at work. This is a principle throughout the Bible. Working hard eventually pays off!

Seek Godly Counsel
The seventh principle is that of seeking Godly counsel. Psalm 1:1 declares:
"Blessed is the man Who walks not in the counsel of the ungodly..."

Proverbs 15:22
"Without counsel, plans go awry, But in the multitude of counsellors they are established."

Before making any major purchase or investment such as buying a house, purchasing a car or just seeking to borrow money for any other purpose, you should first pray about it and then seek the counsel of Godly people. They can keep you from making a lot of mistakes.

The reason so many Saints don't seek Godly counsel before going into money matters is that they don't want to be told by someone that an intended action is unsound—they just like to do what they want anyway.

Above all, don't sign anything until you check the deal thoroughly first. Don't be hurried into any deal. The worst deal in the world is often the one in which a person is rushed into signing—capitulating to a relentless salesman's chance-of-a-lifetime-offer pressure tactics. The best offer in the world can wait.

Chapter Fifteen
LET IT RAIN

Let's revisit Zechariah 10:1-12 NIV
"Ask the LORD for rain In the time of the latter rain. The LORD will make flashing clouds; He will give them showers of rain, Grass in the field for everyone. ² For the idols speak delusion; The diviners envision lies, And tell false dreams; They comfort in vain. Therefore *the people* wend their way like sheep; They are in trouble because *there is* no shepherd. ³ " My anger is kindled against the shepherds, And I will punish the goatherds. *For the LORD of hosts will visit His flock, The house of Judah, And will make them as His royal horse in the battle.* ⁴ *From him comes the cornerstone, From him the tent peg, From him the battle bow, From him every ruler together.* ⁵ *They shall be like mighty men, Who tread down their enemies In the mire of the streets in the battle. They shall fight because the LORD is with them, And the riders on horses shall be put to shame.* ⁶ " *I will strengthen the house of Judah, And I will save the house of Joseph. I will bring them back, Because I have mercy on them. They shall be as though I had not cast them aside For I am the LORD their God, And I will hear them.* ⁷ *Those of Ephraim shall be like a mighty man, And their heart shall rejoice as if*

with wine. Yes, their children shall see *it* and be glad; Their heart shall rejoice in the LORD. [8] I will whistle for them and gather them, For I will redeem them; And they shall increase as they once increased. [9] " I will sow them among the peoples, And they shall remember Me in far countries; They shall live, together with their children, And they shall return. [10] I will also bring them back from the land of Egypt, And gather them from Assyria. I will bring them into the land of Gilead and Lebanon Until no *more room* is found for them. [11] He shall pass through the sea with affliction, And strike the waves of the sea: All the depths of the River shall dry up. Then the pride of Assyria shall be brought down, And the sceptre of Egypt shall depart. [12] " So I will strengthen them in the LORD, And they shall walk up and down in His name," Says the LORD." [Italics added]

Even though it was the time of the Latter Rain, God still commanded that we ask for rain. The word time referred to here is a very interesting Hebrew word and it is a very key word; it is the word Eth.

Eth has two meanings
1. An appointed, set or fixed period that is determined only by God and can only be discerned by His wise sons/daughters.

Wisdom is the ability to discern the Times of God, for example:
Joseph
He was able to accurately discern and interpret the dream that Pharaoh had and as such great success came with it!—Genesis 41:14-36 Fulfilled in Genesis 41:47-57

Daniel
Nebuchadnezzar had a dream, which he could not remember, let alone seek the interpretation. Daniel was able

to recall the dream and to also reveal its interpretation, by the Wisdom of God—Daniel 2:1-45

Then once again Daniel was able to discern and interpret the writings of the Prophets of Israel and know how to birth what was recorded—Daniel 9:2! Another demonstration of the Wisdom of God in action!

The Men Of Issachar
The Bible records that they were able to understand the times and to know exactly what Israel ought to do—1 Chronicles 12:32—once again the Wisdom of God in action...

Second meaning of Eth
2. A proper, suitable or appropriate period of time; for example everything is beautiful in its proper time.

Ecclesiastes 3:11
"He has made everything beautiful in its time. He has also set eternity in the human heart; yet no one can fathom what God has done from beginning to end."

Ask For Rain In The Time Of The Latter Rain
In Israel there were two types of rain—the former and the latter: And they both were always linked together, so it stands to reason that the Lord will immediate respond with the former rain as soon as we sow our seeds! It is then our responsibility to know and discern when it is about to produce a harvest and pray for this Latter Rain!!!

A Former Rain
This fell when the seeds were sown. It was a light rain to moisten the earth so that the seed can germinate.

And A Latter Rain
This rain normally came just before harvest to assist in ripening the crop, the bringing to full maturity the fruit of the tree.

Deuteronomy 11:1-14

"Therefore you shall love the LORD your God, and keep His charge, His statutes, His judgments, and His commandments always. 2 Know today that *I do* not *speak* with your children, who have not known and who have not seen the chastening of the LORD your God, His greatness and His mighty hand and His outstretched arm— 3 His signs and His acts which He did in the midst of Egypt, to Pharaoh king of Egypt, and to all his land; 4 what He did to the army of Egypt, to their horses and their chariots: how He made the waters of the Red Sea overflow them as they pursued you, and *how* the LORD has destroyed them to this day; 5 what He did for you in the wilderness until you came to this place; 6 and what He did to Dathan and Abiram the sons of Eliab, the son of Reuben: how the earth opened its mouth and swallowed them up, their households, their tents, and all the substance that *was* in their possession, in the midst of all Israel— 7 but your eyes have seen every great act of the LORD which He did. 8 "Therefore you shall keep every commandment which I command you today, that you may be strong, and go in and possess the land which you cross over to possess, 9 and that you may prolong *your* days in the land which the LORD swore to give your fathers, to them and their descendants, 'a land flowing with milk and honey.' 10 For the land which you go to possess *is* not like the land of Egypt from which you have come, where you sowed your seed and watered *it* by foot, as a vegetable garden; 11 but the land which you cross over to possess *is* a land of hills and valleys, which drinks water from the rain of heaven, 12 a land for which the LORD your God cares; the eyes of the LORD your God *are* always on it, from the beginning of the year to the very end of the year. [13] 'And it shall be that if you earnestly obey My commandments which I command you today, to love the LORD your God and serve Him with all your heart and with all your soul, [14] then I will give *you* the rain for your land in its season, the early rain and the latter rain, that you may gather in your grain, your new wine, and your oil. [15] And I will send grass in your fields for your livestock, that you may eat and be filled.' [16] Take heed to yourselves, lest your heart be deceived, and you turn aside and serve other gods and worship them, [17] lest the LORD's anger be aroused against you, and He shut up the heavens so that there be no rain, and the land yield no produce, and you perish quickly from the good land which the LORD is giving you."

Joel 2:21-26
"Fear not, O land; Be glad and rejoice, For the LORD has done marvellous things! [22] Do not be afraid, you beasts of the field; For the open pastures are springing up, And the tree bears its fruit; The fig tree and the vine yield their strength. [23] Be glad then, you children And rejoice in the LORD your God; For He has given you the former rain faithfully, And He will cause the rain to come down for you—The former rain, And the latter rain in the first *month.* [24] The threshing floors shall be full of wheat And the vats shall overflow with new wine and oil. [25] " So I will restore to you the years that the swarming locust has eaten, The crawling locust, The consuming locust, And the chewing locust, My great army which I sent among you. [26] You shall eat in plenty and be satisfied, And praise the name of the LORD your God, Who has dealt wondrously with you; And My

people shall never be put to shame. [27] Then you shall know that I *am* in the midst of Israel: I *am* the LORD your God And there is no other. My people shall never be put to shame."

James 5:7-12
"Therefore be patient, brethren, until the coming of the Lord. See *how* the farmer waits for the precious fruit of the earth, waiting patiently for it until it receives the early and latter rain. [8] You also be patient. Establish your hearts, for the coming of the Lord is at hand. [9] Do not grumble against one another, brethren, lest you be condemned.[c] Behold, the Judge is standing at the door! [10] My brethren, take the prophets, who spoke in the name of the Lord, as an example of suffering and patience. [11] Indeed we count them blessed who endure. You have heard of the perseverance of Job and seen the end *intended by* the Lord—that the Lord is very compassionate and merciful. [12] But above all, my brethren, do not swear, either by heaven or by earth or with any other oath. But let your "Yes" be "Yes," and *your* "No," "No," lest you fall into judgment."

However we know that in this particular Scripture God is not speaking about natural rain; the water that comes down from the skies. This rain here is the Revelation, Wisdom, Sound Doctrine, and the very Life of God.

Powerful References: Deuteronomy 32:1-4 and Isaiah 55:10-13

Dealing With Headship First
Whenever God moves for or against a people He deals with the headship first. Leadership is His primary concern.

Here in Zechariah Chapter 10 as God commands us to ask for rain in the time of the Latter Rain, He begins to deal with the Heads; the Shepherds first and speaks judgment against those who have been slack and compromising. *Zechariah 10:2-3a*

"For the idols speak delusion; The diviners envision lies, And tell false dreams; They comfort in vain. Therefore *the people* wend their way like sheep; They are in trouble because *there is* no shepherd. [3] " My anger is kindled against the shepherds, And I will punish the goatherds."

After dealing with the Leaders, the next area He visits is the *House of Judah. Zechariah 10:3b*

"My anger is kindled against the shepherds, And I will punish the goatherds. For the LORD of hosts will visit His flock, The house of Judah, And will make them as His royal horse in the battle."

He then establishes the following from *The House of Judah: Praise*

"From him comes *the cornerstone*, From him the *tent peg*, From him the *battle bow*, From him *every ruler* together."

- His royal horse in battle—Job 39:19-25

- From Judah comes the *cornerstone* [Chief Cornerstone Jesus Christ Himself]

- From Judah comes *the nail or tent peg.* [That is the central part of the tent, on which all others hang; it is the primary place of importance: Praise is very vital in this restorative move of God!]

- Out of Judah [PRAISE] comes the *battle bow*. [Praise stirs up the Lord Sabaoth and it is a weapon of war]

- Out of Judah comes every ruler or oppressor. [It is the Hebrew word *nagas* and it means *despot*, so in essence out of our Praise, oppressors or despots rise up and tread down our enemies, in the mire of the streets.] Zechariah 10:5

Seven Benefits Of The Latter Rain

1. Strength: verse 6

2. Restoration: [bring back] verse 6

3. God will hear: verse 6

4. Rejoicing: verse 7

5. Increase: verse 8

6. Release from Egypt: [worldly systems] verse 10

7. Release form Assyria: [looks successful] verse10

Chapter Sixteen

PASSION FOR ENLARGEMENT: THE BREAKTHROUGH PRAYER OF JABEZ

" " Jabez was more honourable than his brothers. His mother had named him Jabez, saying, "I gave birth to him in pain." 10 Jabez cried out to the God of Israel, "Oh, that you would bless me and enlarge my territory! Let your hand be with me, and keep me from harm so that I will be free from pain." And God granted his request." 1 Chronicles 4:9-10

History shapes the course of our human existence. Today's world, as we know it, exists due to historical events played out in our past. And on a personal level history once again plays a role where often one's past determines patterns of behaviour, thought and lifestyle in the present. Sometimes these patterns carry severe spiritual, psychological and emotional repercussions that may go towards defining a person's identity.

Because these patterns are shaped by the world, they are diametrically opposed to those of the Kingdom of God, and we need to know how to deal with them if we are to be effective in advancing the Kingdom in this hour. We want to look at another young man just like Jacob who violently caused his identity to change and established the purpose of God for his life.

There Is A High Calling—"Honourable" = the Hebrew word for Glory"

The use of the word 'honourable' in verse 9 also has a very interesting application. The same word in the Hebrew, which comes from 'kabad', has one meaning that can be applied in two ways. It means to be heavy, weighty, and severe. The meaning can be applied in a bad sense, as embodied in the opinion of Jabez's mother [representing the world]. It can also be applied in the good sense meaning to be numerous, rich, as well as glorious which was embodied in God's opinion on the matter.

The use of the word suggests that his mother had a deficient understanding of his true purpose for being born. However, within Jabez was [the true kabad] that could have only been perceived by and made manifest in God.

This reveals the "weighty" or "heavy" *Glory* of the *High Calling* and the *Burdensome Price* to pay for it [Philippians 3:12-14, Revelations 14:1-5]!

"Not that I have already obtained all this, or have already arrived at my goal, but I press on to take hold of that for which Christ Jesus took hold of me. 13 Brothers and sisters, I do not consider myself yet to have taken hold of it. But one thing I do: Forgetting what is behind and straining toward what is ahead, 14 I press on toward the goal to win the prize for which God has called me heavenward in Christ Jesus."

"Then I looked, and there before me was the Lamb, standing on Mount Zion, and with him 144,000 who had his name and his Father's name written on their foreheads. 2 And I heard a sound from heaven like the roar of rushing waters and like a loud peal of thunder. The sound I heard was like that of harpists playing their harps. 3 And they sang a new song and the elders. No one could learn the song except the 144,000 who had been redeemed from the earth. 4 These are those who did not defile themselves with women, for they remained virgins. They follow the Lamb wherever he goes. They were purchased from among mankind and offered as first-fruits to God and the Lamb. 5 No lie was found in their mouths; they are blameless."

Jabez knew that by seeking first the Kingdom of God, everything else would be provided. His demands of God were not out of a mere fleshly desire but out of the understanding that the demands would be in line with God's will and therefore would have pleased Him. This is what gave Jabez the legitimacy to violently demand of God a new identity.

Born In Sorrow—"Jabez" = "to grieve, sorrowful; causing pain or travail."

Sorrow = "pain, labour." This reveals the principle of Son-ship as seen in Jesus, "the Man of sorrows" [Isaiah 53:3]; and in His overcoming Brethren who are conformed to His image [Revelations 12:1-5]. Those who know the greatest sorrow and travail of soul shall also know the greatest Joy [for example, women in childbirth—John 16:21; Hebrews 1:9; 12:1-2].

Born In Obscurity—We know nothing of Jabez's history or family. He was known only in the eyes of God; one of God's "are-not's" [1 Corinthians 1:26-31].

"Brothers and sisters, think of what you were when you were called. Not many of you were wise by human standards; not many were influential; not many were of noble birth. 27 But God chose the foolish things of the world to shame the wise; God chose the weak things of the world to shame the strong. 28 God chose the lowly things of this world before the throne and before the four living creatures and the despised things—and the things that are not—to nullify the things that are, 29 so that no one may boast before him. 30 It is because of him that you are in Christ Jesus, who has become for us wisdom from God—that is, our righteousness, holiness and redemption. 31 Therefore, as it is written: "Let the one who boasts boast in the Lord."

The Cry Of Passion—"Called" = "call out or cry out, to utter a loud sound"—"cried out" [NIV].

In verse10, it says that Jabez "called" on the God of Israel. The word called comes from the Hebrew 'qara" which means to call and commission.

It is not a casual petition type prayer but rather a forceful demand made by an apostolic spirit. The word also connotes the idea of accosting a person with whom one has come into contact.

It is the word we use—"Oh" = Passion—intensity and anguish of soul [compare 1 Chronicles 11:17, Job 6:8, 23:3, Psalms 14:7, 107:8, Isaiah 64:1].

In the mind of Jabez, he was not asking for a favour from God but was demanding a right that he knew God wanted to give to him—a new identity.

Two diametrically opposed value systems are at war for the control of the destiny and identity of a human being. The victory of one over the other is determined by the choice of the individual.

It is similar to when Jacob wrestled with God in Genesis 32:22-32 the issue was the same. The blessing that Jacob received from God was one that dealt with the internal issue of reformation. What both Jabez and Jacob understood was that which was articulated by Christ when He says that the Kingdom of God is within [Luke 17:21] and that it suffers violence and the violent take it by force Matthew 11:12!

Only God [this passion is God-ward, directed to God]—Like Jesus, Jabez only wanted what God desired or willed [John 4:34, 5:30, 6:38, 8:29, 15:10, 17:4].

Enlarge My Coasts [Borders]—A Passion For Enlargement!

Enlarge"—"increase; be [or become] great, many, much, numerous; to multiply [used of people, animals, or things]; to make large; to make much to do; to do much." "Coasts" = "a boundary; the territory enclosed: a border, a region" [Exodus 34:24, Deuteronomy 19:8, Psalms 119:31-32, Isaiah 54:2].

Jabez goes on to demonstrate other qualities that allow him to be loosed from his historical fetters.

The Hand Of Discipline [restraint, correction, adjustment]—Psalms 145:15-16, Ephesians 4:11, 1 Peter 5:6.

An Open Hand [representative of the Fivefold Ministry Gifts of Apostles, Prophets, Evangelists, Pastors and Teachers], unlike a Clenched Fist [represented by domineering and over lording], will Mature the Church!

This Hand of Discipline is a Giving, Helping hand! It is a hand of Fellowship [equality]. True Foundational ministry [Ephesians 2:20] is *under*, not *over* you.

That which is Over you Defines and Limits you. Only Jesus can be over you. True ministry Undergirds and Strengthens, envisioning the next generation to be Greater!

"That Your hand would be with me". The use of this phrase comes from the Hebrew word 'hayah', which means to come to pass and which is only used in an emphatic sense. Jabez releases the strength of God into his life with an apostolic decree in order to break the bonds of his historical identity. However, he is not ignorant of the fact that a price needs to be paid in order for the entire process to be fulfilled.

The Evil Of Mediocrity—The word evil comes from 'ra' which means adversity.

"Evil" = "to spoil [literally, by breaking to pieces]; bad, unpleasant, evil [giving pain, unhappiness, misery], distress, injury, calamity."

Grieve = "carve, fabricate, fashion, shape or form; hence, to worry, vex, torture, pain or anger"—to Scar with things ordinary [framed mindsets].

Jabez understood that his [Kingdom] character and identity can only be forged in the violent and courageous confrontation of life. He was willing to face life's circumstances with a victor's mentality rather than a victim's mentality, knowing that God's Hand was in charge of the entire process.

He says "that you would keep me from evil". The word keep comes from the word 'asah' which means to press, to squeeze, to fashion, to make, to produce.

The Answered Cry—"Granted" = "to bring or cause to come in, to gather, bring to pass."

Our God Is "Able" [Romans 4:21, Ephesians 3:20, Philippians 3:21, 2 Timothy 1:12, Hebrews 7:25, Jude 1:24]. His "Oh" is Within us [Galatians 4:6, Colossians 1:27]!

In the statement "God granted him what he requested." The word granted means in the Hebrew to come in, to enter. It connotes the introduction of a new factor into an equation that produces a different result.

Jabez demonstrated such a remarkable response to his human condition that God gives him special mention in the genealogy of the tribe of Judah. Jabez's cry was not made out of a desire to abscond from the responsibility of life but rather to be equipped to wrestle with it victoriously. Jabez accepted the responsibility for personal change. He called on God to become involved in the process. He first discerns the will of God for his life and begins to apostolically decree it into being, violently demanding that God brings His will to pass. Two very important things are to be learnt from Jabez's life!

Firstly, while life subjects all of humanity to its same potentially destructive system, God's involvement, however, ensures that a people committed to advancing the Kingdom of God in their lives will be bettered by the experience and identified by a different name.

Secondly, a Kingdom people are not pushed by a historical past but rather drawn by a prophetic future in God.

Let us be undeterred by any of life's circumstance and boldly forge ahead in the Will, Plan and Purpose of God for our lives as we seek to advance His Kingdom here and now!

Chapter Seventeen

PATIENT ENDURANCE

"In your patience, possess ye your souls." Luke 21:19 [KJV]

Let's take a brief look at "patient endurance" in the Scriptures, and also view it from the perspective of apostolic grace.

Jesus instructed the Apostles in Luke 21:19 "to possess their souls in patience". The backdrop of this instruction was to be one of immense persecution, betrayal by friends and close relatives, hatred and martyrdom. With all these frightful things prophesied in the Apostles' future, Jesus strategy for them to successfully navigate through this time was by means of Patience.

Patience would be the key to the Apostles remaining in control and directing their own souls. Jesus prophesied that they would be beaten in the synagogues and hauled before rulers and Kings and subjected to great injustice. Their challenge during their upcoming trials, as they stood before these men, who had the power and the desire to persecute them [Verse 12], would be to consistently demonstrate the character of Christ in their thoughts, attitudes and responses, firstly toward God; then to themselves and toward their persecutors.

Persecution is possibly the most potent and successful weapon satan has been deploying against all of mankind for centuries. He has had millennia to observe our makeup and implement his machinations, and has become expert in its use. The thing that has made persecution such a powerful strategy for the enemy is that it portends to result in the two things that men fear most. They are pain and loss.

Pain and loss, when allowed to work in our flesh unchecked, provide the enemy with the accesses he desires to our souls. It provides him with the leverage he requires to shift us from our position of completing God's purposes in the earth, to one of despair, destruction and ultimately loss of our reward. The enemy's strategic application of Pain and Loss has caused many a Believer to abandon themselves to angry malicious thoughts, outrage, pride, retaliation, self pity and ultimately blasphemy...[Job 1:11— *"But extend your hand and strike everything he has, and he will no doubt curse you to your face!"*]

Toward the Apostles satan would throw his full arsenal including darts of persecutions and trials. These trials included pain from beatings and torture, pain from betrayal and loss of relationships, pain from imprisonment and banishment, pain from abandonment and humiliation and the ultimate pain of death.

Jesus prophetically gave the Apostles a glimpse into what they would face [Verse 12] and the reason they would have to face it. He also showed them the result that heaven expected out of it. Jesus expected that during their trials and persecution, they would produce "testimonies" [Verse 13]. He expected that, in spite of and through their afflictions, they would be able to be effective witnesses of the truth of the Gospel to everyone they met.

There was to be no forethought, no planning, and no rehearsal of a defence on their part. The natural fleshly reactions that the enemy pressures us to release in times like these were to be kept in check. The Apostles were to present themselves to the Holy Spirit, without any agenda, and without a defence or exit strategy. They would need to possess their souls throughout the ordeal in order for the Holy Spirit to execute God's purpose through them.

But Jesus did not leave them without an example, even in this. Before they were required to endure their own trials, Jesus went through it all, before their very eyes, and by the Holy Spirit, imprinted on their souls what it would take for them to succeed. Jesus was despised and rejected of men [Isaiah 53:3], was falsely accused and did not defend Himself [Isaiah 53:7], and endured the ultimate injustice of a criminal's death on the cross [Hebrews 12:2]. He became their blueprint, and their patient endurance would allow them to interpret and execute God's plans from it.

Patience is translated from the Greek word *hupomone* which means possessing a cheerful or hopeful endurance and constancy, specifically during trials. It is derived from the root word *hupomeno*, which means to endure.

Patience was the ingredient that allowed Jesus to successfully navigate the cross, and is the essential ingredient working in us to empower us to deny ourselves and take up our crosses. Hebrews 12:2 "keeping our eyes fixed on Jesus, the Pioneer and Perfecter of our faith. For the joy set out for Him He endured [*hupomeno*] the cross, disregarding its shame, and *has taken His seat at the right hand of the Throne* of God".

The writer of Hebrews compares the Believer's life to a race [Hebrews 12:1-3]. He did not mean a sprint, which requires speed over a short duration. In sprints, athletes expend their energy in a burst, over a short time, without a great concern for endurance. However, the race he refers to is a marathon. The Greek word used for race is agona from which we derive the word agony. It is also translated as "conflict" and "contention" [Colossians 2:21, 1 Thessalonians 2:2], so we understand from its usage, that the type of race being described requires a tremendous struggle and effort from the participants. And so the Believer's life is not to be considered a walk in the park, but a gruelling fight to the finish.

As marathon runners will tell you, the most significant struggle they face is not from the other participants, or from a hostile environment. Those are realities that the runner has little control over, and the writer in Hebrews also never mentions the presence of others in the race, nor does he describe the immediate environment. The great conflict however...the agony of the race the athlete experiences, is the struggle that takes place on the inside, and the writer in Hebrews parallels this to weights that we must lay aside, and the sin that can easily beset us.

This internal struggle in the athlete manifests itself as the greatest challenge the runner faces in the race, and is something referred to as "hitting the wall". "The wall" usually comes at a critical stage of a marathon between the 20th to 22nd mile of a 26 mile race. The wall hits the athlete as a sudden onset of fatigue and loss of energy that threatens to end the race for them. It is at this point the runner has to make a crucial decision about whether to receive replenishment and press through to the end, or quit the race. The thing that enables the runner to break through the wall and finish the race is Endurance.

Our Lord Jesus faced his wall in the garden of Gethsemane [Mark 14:32-36]

"Then they went to a place called Gethsemane, and Jesus said to his disciples, "Sit here while I pray." 33 He took Peter, James, and John with him, and became very troubled and distressed. 34 He said to them, "My soul is deeply grieved, even to the point of death. Remain here and stay alert." 35 Going a little farther, he threw himself to the ground and prayed that if it were possible the hour would pass from him. 36 He said, "Abba, Father, all things are possible for you. Take this cup away from me. Yet not what I will, but what you will." NET

It was at this point, His strength left Him. His soul was deeply grieved, to the point of dying. It was sheer agony for Him. And, it was at this crucial point, He received replenishment, just like a marathon runner does, and He was able to possess His soul. Luke 22:42-44

"Saying, Father, if thou be willing, remove this cup from me: nevertheless not my will, but thine, be done. 43 And there appeared an angel unto him from heaven, strengthening him. 44 And being in an agony he prayed more earnestly: and his sweat was as it were great drops of blood falling down to the ground." KJV

Never before was it recorded in Scripture that our Lord had felt this way. There was no experience from His past, which He could draw on to prepare Him for this time. It was a critical stage. However, He was able to press through the wall that separated Him from His destiny and that threatened to derail His purpose. He took hold of His soul, endured the agony, and completed the will of God. Hebrews 5:7-9

"During his earthly life Christ offered both requests and supplications, with loud cries and tears, to the one who was able to save him from death and he was heard because of his devotion. 8 Although he was a son, he learned obedience through the things he suffered. 9 And by being perfected in this way, he became the source of eternal salvation to all who obey him," NET

By patiently enduring the suffering of pressing through His wall, Jesus learned obedience. He was perfected or completed, and became the source of eternal salvation for everyone, which was the ultimate plan of the Father.

With this image of Jesus imprinted on their hearts by the Holy Spirit, the Apostles would derive the technology to breakthrough their "walls". Apostle Paul would later write in his letter to the Philippians! Philippians 2:5-8

"Let this mind be in you, which was also in Christ Jesus: 6 Who, being in the form of God, thought it not robbery to be equal with God: 7 But made himself of no reputation, and took upon him the form of a servant, and was made in the likeness of men: 8 And being found in fashion as a man, he humbled himself, and became obedient unto death, even the death of the cross." NET

Jesus disarmed satan of his most potent weapons at Gethsemane and at Calvary. By securing eternal salvation, Jesus procured a magnificent future for all who believe in Him. No longer would the enemy be able to destabilize the Apostles as he had done with Peter at the crucifixion by using the threat of pain and loss of life. From that point on, the Apostles and all who believe on Jesus, have been given a hope that compensates for all they might lose through suffering and trials brought about by the enemy. They have the hope of a blessing, which multiplies and replaces everything satan tries to take away, and also provides an eternity to within which to enjoy it. 2 Corinthians 4:7-18

"But we have this treasure in clay jars, so that the extraordinary power belongs to God and does not come from us. 8 We are experiencing trouble on every side, but are not crushed; we are perplexed, but not driven to despair; 9 we are persecuted, but not abandoned; we are knocked down, but not destroyed, 10 always carrying around in our body the death of Jesus, so that the life of Jesus may also be made visible in our body. 11 For we who are alive are constantly being handed over to death for Jesus' sake, so that the life of Jesus may also be made visible in our mortal body. 12 As a result, death is at work in us, but life is at work in you. 13 But since we have the same spirit of faith as that shown in what has been written, *"I believed; therefore I spoke,"* we also believe, therefore we also speak. 14 We do so because we know that the one who raised up Jesus will also raise us up with Jesus and will bring us with you into his presence. 15 For all these things are for your sake, so that the grace that is including more and more people may cause thanksgiving to increase to the glory of God. 16 Therefore we do not despair, but even if our physical body is wearing away, our inner person is being renewed day by day. 17 For our momentary, light suffering is producing for us an eternal weight of glory far beyond all comparison 18 because we are not looking at what can be seen but at what cannot be seen. For what can be seen is temporary, but what cannot be seen is eternal." NET

"And Peter said, "Look, we have left everything we own to follow you!" 29 Then Jesus said to them, "I tell you the truth, there is no one who has left home or wife or brothers or parents or children for the sake of God's kingdom 30 who will not receive many times more in this age – and in the age to come, eternal life." Luke 18:28-30 NET

"Then Peter said to him, "Look, we have left everything to follow you! What then will there be for us?" 28 Jesus said to them, "I tell you the truth: In the age when all things are renewed, when the Son of Man sits on his glorious throne, you who have followed me will also sit on twelve thrones, judging the twelve tribes of Israel. 29 And whoever has left houses or brothers or sisters or father or mother or children or fields for my sake will receive a hundred times as much and will inherit eternal life." Mathew 19:27-29 NET

However, the Apostles understood, that despite the great and precious promises made available to them, that the key to accessing the promise, which lay at the end of their trials, was endurance. Without the ability to endure to the end, there would be no prize. Just like in the case of a marathon runner, without patient endurance through the "wall" there is no victory. [Matthew 10:22]

"But remember the former days when you endured a harsh conflict of suffering after you were enlightened. 33 At times you were publicly exposed to abuse and afflictions, and at other times you came to share with others who were treated in that way. 34 For in fact you shared the sufferings of those in prison, and you accepted the confiscation of your belongings with joy, because you knew that you certainly had a better and lasting possession. 35 So do not throw away your confidence, because it has great reward. 36 For you need endurance in order to do God's will and so receive what is promised. 37 For *just a little longer* and *he who is coming will arrive and not delay. But my righteous one will live by faith, and if he shrinks back, I take no pleasure in him.* But we are not among those who shrink back and thus perish, but are among those who have faith and preserve their souls." Hebrews 10:32-39 NET

In Hebrews 12:1-3 and James 1:4 we see four dimensions of apostolic grace that can become ours through the technology of patience!

1. The Ability To Decode The Plans Of God—Patience allows us to decode and apply the blueprint for God's plan for our lives, which is to be built up in Christ [Colossians 2:7] and be conformed to Christ (Romans 12:2). This is expressed in James 1:4 as us being "perfect and complete and not deficient". Patience, when allowed to work in us, completes the work of God in building us up into Christ, both individually and corporately as the Body of Christ

2. Finishing Ability—in Hebrews 12:2 Patience [endurance] is what enabled Jesus to become the "Finisher of the faith". It is the key to finishing the work God has given us, and not becoming ruined by the schemes of the enemy. The enemy often uses a 3 step descending ladder to erect a wall in our life to derail us. These steps are:
   a. Mumbling within ourselves!

   b. Complaining to others and

   c. Open rebellion against the Purposes of God!

However, patience keeps us constantly on track!

3. Ability To Persevere—Patience gives us the ability to persevere by taking away the "sting of the trial or persecution", which is pain and the suffering of loss!

   - Patience offers us the opportunity to acquire something much more valuable than what we will lose.

   - Patience guarantees maturity and conformity to the character of Christ—James 1:2

- You will be rewarded and receive the tender mercies of God—James 5:11

- Patience is needed to attain the promise—Hebrews 10:36

4. Maintain Focus—Patient endurance allows us to keep our focus on the goal of God's purpose and run the race in spite of obstacles [Hebrews 10:36]

Jesus understood that His temporary loss would result in His ultimate gain. We also learn through patient endurance, as Job did, that God is tender and merciful and will remove the sting of loss, and bless us in the end. Patience is a vital part of the process that enables God to work over a long span of time, if needed, to produce in us the image of Christ so that we "may be perfect and complete", lacking nothing.

Chapter Eighteen
THE RESURRECTION
TO LIVE FOR I

As I bring this volume to a close I would like to offer you a chapter from one of my previously published book titled "Leaven Revealed".

The subject that I am about to broach is one of increasing conflict and debate between certain camps in Christendom and as such I know it could be very controversial to some. I ask that you not just read the pages of this book but to also study.

From the onset, I would like to go on record and say that the Resurrection has nothing to do with our spirits or souls but only our physical bodies—would you agree with this? That this Resurrection of the body is one of the major pillars of the Christian Faith! That when we as Believers, currently die our spirits and soul go to be with the Lord but our bodies remain in the grave or tomb or wherever and rot and that, that same body will be resurrected to put on immortality and in-corruption [that very same body, not a different one]... The Resurrection is that of the dead and there are two types, there's a resurrection of the *just* and of the *unjust*. Belief in the resurrection from the dead is central to the Christian faith.

Here is what Jesus Christ said as He walked the face of the earth.

"Verily, verily, I say unto you, The hour is coming, and now is, when the dead shall hear the voice of the Son of God: and they that hear shall live. For as the Father hath life in himself; so hath he given to the Son to have life in himself; And hath given him authority to execute judgment also, because he is the Son of man. Marvel not at this: for the hour is coming, in the which all that are in the graves shall hear his voice, And shall come forth; they that have done *good*, unto the *resurrection of life*; and they that have done *evil*, unto the *resurrection of damnation*." [Italics added] John 5:25-29

Here is what the early Apostles said as they walked the face of the earth.

"However, I admit that I worship the God of our fathers as a follower of the Way, which they call a sect. I believe everything that agrees with the Law and that is written in the Prophets, [15]and *I have the same hope in God as these men, that there will be a resurrection of both the righteous and the wicked.* [16]So I strive always to keep my conscience clear before God and man." [Italics added] Acts 24:14-16

[12]But if it is preached that Christ has been raised from the dead, how can some of you say that there is no resurrection of the dead? [13]If there is no resurrection of the dead, then not even Christ has been raised. [14]And if Christ has not been raised, our preaching is useless and so is your faith. [15]More than that, we are then found to be false witnesses about God, for we have testified about God that he raised Christ from the dead. But he did not raise him if in fact the dead are not raised. [16]For if the dead are not raised, then Christ has not been raised either. [17]And if Christ has not been raised, your

faith is futile; you are still in your sins. [18]Then those also who have fallen asleep in Christ are lost. [19]If only for this life we have hope in Christ, we are to be pitied more than all men. [20]But Christ has indeed been raised from the dead, the firstfruits of those who have fallen asleep. [21]For since death came through a man, the resurrection of the dead comes also through a man. [22]For as in Adam all die, so in Christ all will be made alive. [23]But each in his own turn: Christ, the firstfruits; then, when he comes, those who belong to him. [24]Then the end will come, when he hands over the kingdom to God the Father after he has destroyed all dominion, authority and power. [25]For he must reign until he has put all his enemies under his feet. [26]The last enemy to be destroyed is death. [27]For he "has put everything under his feet."[a] Now when it says that "everything" has been put under him, it is clear that this does not include God himself, who put everything under Christ. [28]When he has done this, then the Son himself will be made subject to him who put everything under him, so that God may be all in all. [29]Now if there is no resurrection, what will those do who are baptized for the dead? If the dead are not raised at all, why are people baptized for them? [30]And as for us, why do we endanger ourselves every hour? 1 Corinthians 15:12-30

For those of you who may be having a debate as to whether the Resurrection is a valid experience and as such to be hoped for, I would like to begin a chapter from my recent book "Leaven Revealed" where I dealt with the leaven of the Sadducees a religious sect in Jesus Christ's day who did not believe in the Resurrection.

The Sadducees were another priestly group and some Christians probably lump them together with the Pharisees as they are often mentioned together in the Bible. But the

Sadducees were very different from the Pharisees as they were descendants of Aaron and associated with the leadership of the Temple in Jerusalem. Of note, during Jesus Christ's time on earth the religious/political group of the Sadducees was known for their liberalism. They were very aristocratic and tended to be very wealthy and held very powerful positions, such as that of high priest.

The Sadducees held the majority of the 70 seats of the ruling council known as the [3]Sanhedrin. They moved with the "upper class" of society and mirrored many of Rome's political maneuvers to gain strength and popularity among the Roman authorities. To their own advancement, they also worked very closely with the Pharisee minority in the Sanhedrin council as the Pharisees had the hearts of the common folk. This worked in tandem to their advantage as the Sadducees had the hearts of the affluent.

The Sadducees held fast to the written Word of God—especially the Pentateuch, which is comprised of Genesis through Deuteronomy and is also known as the Five Books of Moses. However, due to their extremely political bias they tended to compromise Scripture and adopted some erroneous doctrinal practices and beliefs. As a matter of fact these religious zealots of the day were the ones who with the Pharisees plotted to crucify Jesus Christ when their authority was severely being threatened by His teachings.

"Then the Pharisees and Sadducees came, and testing Him asked that He would show them a sign

---

[3] A variety of theories have developed concerning the Sanhedrin of Jewish leaders in Jerusalem. The three most prevalent are that the Sanhedrin was composed of political leaders, including some priests and aristocrats; that the Sanhedrin was composed of religious leaders knowledgeable in the law, including priests, Pharisees, and scribes; and that there were two Sanhedrins, one political and the other religious. Achtemeier, Paul J., Th.D., Harper's Bible Dictionary, (San Francisco: Harper and Row, Publishers, Inc.) 1985.

from heaven. [2]He answered and said to them, "When it is evening you say, 'It will be fair weather, for the sky is red'; [3]and in the morning, 'It will be foul weather today, for the sky is red and threatening.' Hypocrites! You know how to discern the face of the sky, but you cannot discern the signs of the times. [4]A wicked and adulterous generation seeks after a sign, and no sign shall be given to it except the sign of the prophet Jonah." And He left them and departed. [5]Now when His disciples had come to the other side, they had forgotten to take bread. [6]Then Jesus said to them, "Take heed and beware of the leaven of the Pharisees and the Sadducees." [7]And they reasoned among themselves, saying, "It is because we have taken no bread." [8]But Jesus, being aware of it, said to them, "O you of little faith, why do you reason among yourselves because you have brought no bread? [9]Do you not yet understand, or remember the five loaves of the five thousand and how many baskets you took up? [10]Nor the seven loaves of the four thousand and how many large baskets you took up? [11]How is it you do not understand that I did not speak to you concerning bread?–but to beware of the leaven of the Pharisees and Sadducees." [12]Then they understood that He did not tell them to beware of the leaven of bread, but of the doctrine of the Pharisees and Sadducees. Matthew 16:1-12

"The same day the Sadducees, *who say there is no resurrection*, came to Him with a question. [24]"Teacher," they said, "Moses told us that if a man dies without having children, his brother must marry the widow and have children for him. [25]Now there were seven brothers among us. The first one married and died, and since he had no children, he left his wife to his brother. [26]The same thing happened to the second and third brother, right on down to the seventh. ^{27}Finally, the woman died. ^{28}Now then, at the resurrection, whose wife will she be of the seven, since all of them were married to her?" ^{29}Jesus replied, "You are in error because you do not know the Scriptures or the power of God. ^{30}At the resurrection people will neither marry nor be given in marriage; they will be like the angels in heaven. ^{31}But about the resurrection of the dead—have you not read what God said to you, ^{32}'I am the God of Abraham, the God of Isaac, and the God of Jacob'? He is not the God of the dead but of the living." ^{33}When the crowds heard this, they were astonished at his teaching." [Italics added] Matthew 22:23-33

According to Matthew 16:1-12 and 22:23 the Sadducees did not believe in the resurrection of the dead or the immortality of the soul, yet they questioned Jesus on aspects of the Scripture denoting the resurrection. They were conniving all the while to trap Jesus!

They did not believe in rewards or punishments being handed out after death. Hence they denied the doctrines of Heaven and hell. The Sadducees were legalists and held their people in bondage to the Law.

I believe that there were four main areas of leaven or contradictions to Scripture that the Sadducees functioned in that we need to be aware of. They are:

- They denied the Resurrection of the dead.

- They denied the existence of angels and demons—Acts 23:6-8.

- They denied life after death, proclaiming that the soul perished at death and as such there was neither reward, nor penalty for things done in one's earthly life.

- They were very self-centered and self-sufficient and as such denied the Lord's involvement in their day-to-day lives.

Of the four main areas of error or leaven that the Sadducees subscribed to, their unbelief in the Resurrection of the dead was the most deadly and as such we will need to explore this aspect in a bit more detail.

The Resurrection Of The Dead

This is a very elaborate and extensive study and the scope of this writing is not intended to explore such depth. However, as we briefly touch on this subject let me state that the Resurrection is one of the foundational pillars of the Gospel and the Christian Church!

The Resurrection was so important that it was one of the main topics of the early Apostles' teachings. When they preached they always testified concerning the Resurrection of Jesus Christ, and the consequent resurrection of the dead. As a matter of fact the Resurrection of Jesus Christ in bodily form was so important that when the remaining Eleven Apostles had to chose another Apostle to replace Judas Iscariot who had became apostate, they knew that the replacement had to have witnessed the Resurrection of Jesus Christ.

"In those days Peter stood up among the believers (a group numbering about a hundred and twenty) [16]and said, "Brothers, the Scripture had to be fulfilled which the Holy Spirit spoke long ago through the mouth of David concerning Judas, who served as guide for those who arrested Jesus— [17]he was one of our number and shared in this ministry." [18](With the reward he got for his wickedness, Judas bought a field; there he fell headlong, his body burst open and all his intestines spilled out. [19]Everyone in Jerusalem heard about this, so they called that field in their language Akeldama, that is, Field of Blood.) [20]"For," said Peter, "it is written in the book of Psalms, " 'May his place be deserted; let there be no one to dwell in it,' and, " 'May another take his place of leadership.'

21Therefore it is necessary to choose one of the men who have been with us the whole time the Lord Jesus went in and out among us, 22beginning from John's baptism to the time when Jesus was taken up from us. *For one of these must become a witness with us of his resurrection."* 23So they proposed two men: Joseph called Barsabbas (also known as Justus) and Matthias. 24Then they prayed, "Lord, you know everyone's heart. Show us which of these two you have chosen 25to take over this apostolic ministry, which Judas left to go where he belongs." 26Then they cast lots, and the lot fell to Matthias; so he was added to the eleven apostles." [Italics added] Acts 1:15-26

From that time the Apostles continued to preach very strongly concerning the Resurrection of the dead. We see this in the following Scriptural texts.

When Apostle Peter stood up before the multitude, he declared unto them that "David spoke of the Resurrection of Jesus Christ." When Peter and John were taken before the council, after healing the man at the Temple gate, the great cause of their arrest was not because of that healing as some may suppose. No, the rulers were grieved because they propagated the teachings of Jesus Christ including the Resurrection from the dead.

"The priests and the captain of the temple guard and the Sadducees came up to Peter and John while they were speaking to the people. 2They were greatly disturbed because the apostles were teaching the people and proclaiming in Jesus the resurrection of the dead. 3They seized Peter and John, and because it was evening, they put them in jail until the next day." Acts 4:1-3

Even the caging of Peter and John as criminals in a common jail did not diminish the Apostles' fervour about preaching on the resurrection from the dead. When they were set free, after having been examined, they returned to the brethren and gave their report as we read in the following: "²³On their release, Peter and John went back to their own people and reported all that the chief priests and elders had said to them... ³³With great power the apostles continued to testify to the resurrection of the Lord Jesus, and much grace was upon them all." Acts 4:23, 33.

It was the resurrection which stirred the curiosity of the Athenians when Apostle Paul preached among them:

"While Paul was waiting for them in Athens, he was greatly distressed to see that the city was full of idols. ¹⁷So he reasoned in the synagogue with the Jews and the God-fearing Greeks, as well as in the marketplace day by day with those who happened to be there. ¹⁸A group of Epicurean and Stoic philosophers began to dispute with him. Some of them asked, "What is this babbler trying to say?" Others remarked, "He seems to be advocating foreign gods." They said this because Paul was preaching the good news *about Jesus and the resurrection.* Then they took him and brought him to a meeting of the Areopagus, where they said to him, "May we know what this new teaching is that you are presenting?" [Italics added] Acts 17:16-19

In response to them the Apostle Paul preached the Gospel with fervour and ended on the note concerning the Resurrection of the dead. This moved the Areopagites to respond in a scornful and contemptuous manner, as we see in the following Scripture Reference:

"When they heard about the resurrection of the dead, some of them sneered, but others said, "We want to hear you again on this subject." Acts 4:32

As the Apostle Paul was nearing the end of his life on earth, he was arrested in Jerusalem and was brought before the Sanhedrin Council as Rome could not find any fault with him. Remember that Apostle Paul was a Roman citizen and ill treatment of a Roman citizen could have serious consequences on the person making the allegations and imposing the sentence.

> "Those who were about to question him withdrew immediately. The commander himself was alarmed when he realized that he had put Paul, a Roman citizen, in chains.[30]The next day, since the commander wanted to find out exactly why Paul was being accused by the Jews, he released him and ordered the chief priests and all the Sanhedrin to assemble. Then he brought Paul and had him stand before them." Acts 22:29-30

Without fear of man, not even the ruling party of the Sanhedrin Council and the high priest, he rose up in only the way Apostle Paul could and stated the following:

> "Paul looked straight at the Sanhedrin and said, "My brothers, I have fulfilled my duty to God in all good conscience to this day." ...[6]Then Paul, knowing that some of them were Sadducees and the others Pharisees, called out in the Sanhedrin, "My brothers, I am a Pharisee, the son of a Pharisee. *I stand on trial because of my hope in the resurrection of the dead.*"
> [7]When he said this, a dispute broke out between the Pharisees and the Sadducees, and the assembly was divided. [8](The Sadducees say that there is no resurrection, and that there are neither angels nor spirits, but the Pharisees acknowledge them all.)"
> [Italics added] Acts 23:1, 6-8

Chapter Nineteen

THE RESURRECTION TO LIVE FOR II

W hen we speak about the Resurrection of the dead we are not speaking about one's spirit or soul as these are already eternal. However, our physical body [the body consisting of flesh, blood and bones] in the current state is *not* eternal.

As we study Scripture we would all have to agree that regardless to our doctrinal position one thing is certain, God's original plan was and still is, His desire and ultimate goal to have earth populated with mankind [by mankind we mean, a being with a spirit and a soul who live in a body of flesh]. We are not going to live in Heaven. God never intended for mankind to live in Heaven. It was and still is His desire and intent for us to live on planet earth! However having said that, in order for that to be accomplished we must have bodies that can fulfill that objective, hence the reason for the Resurrection. Our current bodies will have to put on immortality in order for us [spirit and soul] to live forever on planet earth.

Let me once again re-emphasize that the Resurrection is not a simple concept or occurrence, it is the very basis for the Christian Faith. The Old Testament Saints believed in it and longed and looked forward for it. The Book of Hebrews records a powerful point in support of this when the writer penned the following by the inspiration of the Holy Spirit:

"Now faith is being sure of what we hope for and certain of what we do not see. [2]This is what the ancients were commended for... [13]All these people were still living by faith when they died. They did not receive the things promised; they only saw them and welcomed them from a distance. And they admitted that they were aliens and strangers on earth. [14]People who say such things show that they are looking for a country of their own. [15]If they had been thinking of the country they had left, they would have had opportunity to return. [16]Instead, they were longing for a better country—a heavenly one. Therefore God is not ashamed to be called their God, for he has prepared a city for them... [20]By faith Isaac blessed Jacob and Esau in regard to their future. [21]By faith Jacob, when he was dying, blessed each of Joseph's sons, and worshiped as he leaned on the top of his staff. *[22]By faith Joseph, when his end was near, spoke about the exodus of the Israelites from Egypt and gave instructions about his bones...* [32]And what more shall I say? I do not have time to tell about Gideon, Barak, Samson, Jephthah, David, Samuel and the prophets, [33]who through faith conquered kingdoms, administered justice, and gained what was promised; who shut the mouths of lions, [34]quenched the fury of the flames, and escaped the edge of the sword; whose weakness was turned to strength; and who became powerful in battle and routed foreign armies. [35]Women received back their dead, raised to life again. Others were tortured and refused to be released, so that they might gain a better resurrection. [36]Some faced jeers and flogging, while still others were chained and put in prison. [37]They were stoned; they were sawed in two; they were put to death by the sword. They went about in sheepskins and goatskins, destitute, persecuted and mistreated—38the world was not worthy of them. They wandered in deserts and mountains, and in caves and holes in the ground. 39These were all commended for their faith, yet none of them received what had been promised. 40God had planned something better for us so that only together with us would they be made perfect. [Italics added] Hebrews 11:1-2, 13-40

Verse 22 reveals that—By faith Joseph, when his end was near, spoke about the exodus of the Israelites from Egypt and gave instructions about his bones—therein lies one of the most powerful truths concerning the Resurrection. Instruction about the care of a person's bones seems like a strange thing to record about a man in Hebrews Chapter 11, known as the Faith Chapter in Scripture. It makes you wonder why Joseph's bones were mentioned at all. After all, the Chapter speaks to the faith of the Patriarchs and the hurdles they had to pass through. So, what does the mention of a dead person's bones have to do with faith? To fully understand this we need to briefly retrace the life of this great Patriarch along with some of his Kinsmen.

The entire 23rd Chapter of Genesis deals with Abraham purchasing a cave for the burial of his wife and family. The resting place for the remains of his relatives was very important and sacred to Abraham. Sarah died and it was time to provide a final resting place for his loved ones. Abraham refused to take it as a gift and required that the deal be signed and sealed so that future generations could not deny that this place belonged to Abraham and his heirs.

Abraham, the Bible says, was a Prophet and through the eyes of faith, he saw the future unfold. He knew that one day, the very land he was adamant in purchasing as a burial ground would belong to the tribe of Judah, just a few miles south of Jerusalem, the Holy City.

Later on in time Jacob, Abraham's grandson is about to die and he calls all his sons to himself and instructs and blesses them before his departure as recorded in Genesis:

"Then he gave them these instructions: "I am about to be gathered to my people. Bury me with my fathers in the cave in the field of Ephron the Hittite, 30 the cave in the field of Machpelah, near Mamre in Canaan, which Abraham bought as a burial place from Ephron the Hittite, along with the field. 31 There Abraham and his wife Sarah were buried, there Isaac and his wife Rebekah were buried, and there I buried Leah. 32 The field and the cave in it were bought from the Hittites." Genesis 49:29-32

Abraham's cave at Machpelah not only held the remains of Abraham and Sarah, but also Isaac, Rebekah, Jacob and Leah. They all rested in this place and now, much later in time and a long ways away in the land of Egypt we find Joseph giving instructions for his bones to be taken out with the children of Israel when God brought them out of Egypt. He declared to the Israelites:

"Then Joseph said to his brothers, "I am about to die. But God will surely come to your aid and take you up out of this land to the land he promised on oath to Abraham, Isaac and Jacob." 25And Joseph made the sons of Israel swear an oath and said, "*God will surely come to your aid, and then you must carry my bones up from this place.*" 26So Joseph died at the age of a hundred and ten. And after they embalmed him, he was placed in a coffin in Egypt." [Italics added] Genesis 50:24-26

Joseph died and his body was embalmed and placed in a tomb in Egypt for hundreds of years. The Children of Israel continued in their hellish bondage and one has to pose the question as to how many of them really believed Joseph's prophetic insight in declaring that they would be liberated. Hundreds of years passed and his prophecy that declared that God would bring them out should have given them incredible faith and hope.

"And Moses took the bones of Joseph with Him." [Exodus 13:19] He was taking no chances. The Word of God had been spoken, and an oath had been taken. Moses knew that the impossible task before him could only be met through the Word of God. His strength and abilities were as nothing in the face of the problem, but this coffin of bones was his insurance. Joseph, the Prophet of God, had spoken the word. And Moses stood on the word of God.

The Resurrection was so important to Joseph that his body remained in a tomb in Egypt for over 400 years and then was transported through the wilderness for another 40 years before finally coming to rest in the Promised Land.

One may ask what difference could it possibly make to Joseph where his dead body rested? The answer is that he was a very spiritual man, and as long as he knew his spirit would be with his Lord, why was he so concerned about his flesh? It was far more than just a sentimental gesture. There was a deep spiritual significance.

Joseph was a Prophet, a Seer, one who sees future events. And he saw a glorious event taking place more than seventeen centuries after his death. He saw the glory that would come to those who would be able to participate in this great event, and he wanted to be a part of it. Hear me beloved, for this concerns you today. The Spirit of God showed this man a glory that was coming. But there was something he had to do. He made arrangements for his body to be buried just south of the city of Jerusalem, in a cave purchased for that very purpose. He made provisions to be in the place where he could participate in the greatest event ever where Jesus Christ gave Himself to be a blood sacrifice to redeem us from sin and Joseph knew that many years hence, he too would partake in that glory.

This wonderful event is recorded in the Gospel of Matthew:

"And when Jesus had cried out again in a loud voice, he gave up his spirit. [51]At that moment the curtain of the temple was torn in two from top to bottom. The earth shook and the rocks split. [52]The tombs broke open and the bodies of many holy people who had died were raised to life. [53]They came out of the tombs, and after Jesus' resurrection they went into the holy city and appeared to many people." Matthew 27:51-53

What a world shaking, history-making thing was taking place! Jesus Christ had been crucified, had paid the penalty for our sins, and on the third day had risen from the tomb. Matthew reports that the moment Jesus Christ cried out with a loud voice and died that the veil in the Old Covenant Temple was torn from top to bottom [signifying the end to the old system], and that many Saints who previously died and were buried, were resurrected. And for three days they remained alive in their tombs. Then, following His resurrection, graves of many of the saints were opened and they came into the city. Although the Scriptures do not specify the names of all who were resurrected, I am confident that some of them were mentioned in Hebrews Chapter 11. Possibly Joseph was among those who were resurrected!

It states that "They went into the city," so it stands to reason that the graves were somewhere outside the city. It does not say where the graves were, but I know of one that was located in a cave somewhere south of Jerusalem, which

I am confident you would find empty if you went there today. They "appeared unto many." It does not say they were recognized, but they were seen. They were not seen as spirits or ghosts, not as dried up piles of bones rattling down the streets of Jerusalem, but they were seen in their bodies, their new bodies, their *Resurrected, Glorified Bodies*. And nowhere does it say, and it would be a violation of Scripture and reason to even imagine that those Saints returned to their old graves and died again or returned to dust.

I believe with all my heart that the Prophet Joseph was among those who walked the streets of Jerusalem that day, as well as Abraham, Isaac, and Jacob. Why else did the Spirit lead them to make their burial place certain, almost on the outskirts of that city where all this was taking place? So what is the result? Many bodies of Saints, including all the New Testament Church who have gone on to be with the Lord are still in the grave today, waiting for the Resurrection. Then shall they be clothed upon with life, and then shall death be swallowed up in victory! This is our inheritance as Saints, and we are looking ever onward to that blessed hope.

But there were some who did not have to wait until the final trump for their corruptible bodies to put on incorruptible. Up to now, they have been enjoying their glorified bodies for almost 2000 years. Why? Because they were men and women of faith, Saints, "set apart."

Consider again Joseph. While he had the authority, he made them take an oath so binding upon Israel that in spite of the difficulties involved, they had to carry his bones through 40 years of wilderness wanderings until they could put him to rest in the Cave. By the eye of the Spirit he not only saw the departure of the Children of Israel from Egypt, but he also saw a greater event and made sure that he would be near enough to be a part of it.

The important thing about this whole message is how it affects us today in this end of the age. I want you to see the glorious thing that God is about to do in the earth in our time. The Saints who arose with Jesus Christ were the first-fruits of the Resurrection. They are living proof that the harvest is actually going to follow. We do not have to fear that this glorious promise of life after death is only a myth or fable. Jesus Christ Himself with many of the Saints actually arose and walked the streets of Jerusalem in their new bodies and were seen by the people. This was the first-fruits, but the harvest was to wait for many centuries. Joseph did not have to wait; he could be in the first-fruits company, because of his vision, his desire, and his faith. God has promised that the "latter house shall be greater than the former."

Let the bones of Joseph speak to your heart; he [well his bones] spent over 1700 years in a tomb waiting for the Messiah to come, to die, be buried and to rise again from the dead so that he could have experienced the First Resurrection or to be among the First-Fruits of them who slept. Well there still remains a Resurrection of the body for those Saints who have died and will die before Jesus Christ returns to finally setup His Throne and headquarters upon planet earth!

I believe that there is a final Resurrection still to be accomplished. Some will be resurrected to eternal damnation and others to eternal life and bliss. Even though we have been waiting a little under 2000 years to see this happen, I am here to tell you that it certainly will happen!

There are some who have been locked into this doctrine of the Sadducees and are denying any resurrection to come. However, there must be a final Resurrection as God will come and permanently live upon the earth!

When Jesus Christ came in the flesh the first time, He came as Saviour to die for the sins of the world. At that time the Jews wanted Him to set up His Kingdom with them and overthrow the Roman rule. He rejected that as He was on a mission to die for the sins of the world. However, when He returns He will be coming as King of His Kingdom to reign forever in the earth.

There is so much more that can be said about the Resurrection, that it will take many, many more books to completely deal with this all-important pillar of the Christian Faith. However, I would like to leave you with the following all-important passage from one of Apostle Paul's letters to the Corinthian church concerning the Resurrection:

"Now, brothers, I want to remind you of the gospel I preached to you, which you received and on which you have taken your stand. ^{2}By this gospel you are saved, if you hold firmly to the word I preached to you. Otherwise, you have believed in vain. ^{3}For what I received I passed on to you as of first importance: that Christ died for our sins according to the Scriptures, ^{4}that he was buried, that he was raised on the third day according to the Scriptures, ^{5}and that he appeared to Peter, and then to the Twelve. ^{6}After that, he appeared to more than five hundred of the brothers at the same time, most of whom are still living, though some have fallen asleep. ^{7}Then he appeared to James, then to all the apostles, ^{8}and last of all he appeared to me also, as to one abnormally born. ^{9}For I am the least of the apostles and do not even deserve to be called an apostle, because I persecuted the church of God. ^{10}But by the grace of God I am what I am, and his grace to me was not without effect. No, I worked harder than all of them—yet not I, but the grace of God that was with me. ^{11}Whether, then, it was I or they, this is what we preach, and this is what you believed. *^{12}But if it is preached that Christ has been raised from the dead,* *how can some of you say that there is no resurrection of the dead?* [13]*If there is no resurrection of the dead, then not even Christ has been raised.* [14]And if Christ has not been raised, our preaching is useless and so is your faith. [15]More than that, we are then found to be false witnesses about God, for we have testified about God that he raised Christ from the dead. But he did not raise him if in fact the dead are not raised. [16]*For if the dead are not raised, then Christ has not been raised either.* [17]And if Christ has not been raised, your faith is futile; you are still in your sins. [18]*Then those also who have fallen asleep in Christ are lost.* [19]If only for this life we have hope in Christ, we are to be pitied more than all men. [20]But Christ has indeed been raised from the dead, the first-fruits of those who have fallen asleep. [21]For since death came through a man, the resurrection of the dead comes also through a man. [22]For as in Adam all die, so in Christ all will be made alive. [23]But each in his own turn: Christ, the first-fruits; then, when he comes, those who belong to him. [24]Then the end will come, when he hands over the kingdom to God the Father after he has destroyed all dominion, authority and power. [25]For he must reign until he has put all his enemies under his feet. [26]The last enemy to be destroyed is death. [27]For he "has put everything under his feet." Now when it says that "everything" has been put under him, it is clear that this does not include God himself, who put everything under Christ. [28]When he has done this, then the Son himself will be made subject to him who put everything under him, so that God may be all in all. [29]Now if there is no resurrection, what will those do who are baptized for the dead? If the dead are not raised at all, why are people baptized for them? 30And as for us, why do we endanger ourselves every hour? 31I die every day—I mean that, brothers—just as surely as I glory over you in Christ Jesus our Lord. 32If I fought wild beasts in Ephesus for merely human reasons, what have I gained? If the dead are not raised, "Let us eat and drink, for tomorrow we die." 33Do not be misled: "Bad company corrupts good character." 34Come back to your senses as you ought, and stop sinning; for there are some who are ignorant of God—I say this to your shame. 35But someone may ask, "How are the dead raised? With what kind of body will they come?" 36How foolish! What you sow does not come to life unless it dies. 37When you sow, you do not plant the body that will be, but just a seed, perhaps of wheat or of something else. 38But God gives it a body as he has determined, and to each kind of seed he gives its own body. 39All flesh is not the same: Men have one kind of flesh, animals have another, birds another and fish another. 40There are also heavenly bodies and there are earthly bodies; but the splendour of the heavenly bodies is one kind, and the splendour of the earthly bodies is another. 41The sun has one kind of splendour, the moon another and the stars another; and star differs from star in splendour. *42So will it be with the resurrection of the dead. The body that is sown is perishable, it is raised imperishable; 43it is sown in dishonour, it is raised in glory; it is sown in weakness, it is raised in power; 44it is sown a natural body, it is raised a spiritual body. If there is a natural body, there is also a spiritual body.* 45So it is written: "The first man Adam became a living being"; the last Adam, a life-giving spirit. 46The spiritual did not come first, but the natural, and after that the spiritual.

^{47}The first man was of the dust of the earth, the second man from heaven. ^{48}As was the earthly man, so are those who are of the earth; and as is the man from heaven, so also are those who are of heaven. ^{49}And just as we have borne the likeness of the earthly man, so shall we bear the likeness of the man from heaven. ^{50}I declare to you, brothers, that flesh and blood cannot inherit the kingdom of God, nor does the perishable inherit the imperishable. ^{51}Listen, I tell you a mystery: We will not all sleep, but we will all be changed— ^{52}in a flash, in the twinkling of an eye, at the last trumpet. For the trumpet will sound, the dead will be raised imperishable, and we will be changed. *^{53}For the perishable must clothe itself with the imperishable, and the mortal with immortality. ^{54}When the perishable has been clothed with the imperishable, and the mortal with immortality, then the saying that is written will come true: "Death has been swallowed up in victory."* ^{55}"Where, O death, is your victory? Where, O death, is your sting?" ^{56}The sting of death is sin, and the power of sin is the law. ^{57}But thanks be to God! He gives us the victory through our Lord Jesus Christ. ^{58}Therefore, my dear brothers, stand firm. Let nothing move you. Always give yourselves fully to the work of the Lord, because you know that your labour in the Lord is not in vain." [Italics added] 1 Corinthians 15:1-58

As we have seen in this chapter, the Sadducees were legalists and held their people in bondage to the Law with no hope in the promises of Scripture. This proved to be a very powerful control tactic to the religious faithful who succumbed to tradition and who did not have independent thoughts on the matter. The leaven of the Sadducees was "legalism and unbelief in the Resurrection", and in their day, they managed to have it leaven and corrupt the whole loaf of the Jewish society, but only until Jesus Christ arrived!

DOMINION-LIFE
INTERNATIONAL MINISTRIES

CANADA | USA
P.O. Box 44078 Kensington SQ
Burnaby, BC, V5B 4Y2
Canada

P.O. Box 1817
Ferndale, WA
98248, USA

TEL: 778-859-6752 | FAX: 604-291-7015

Website: dominion-life.org

KINGDOM-IMPACT INTERNATIONAL NETWORK
Website: http://kinternationalnetwork.org/

OTHER EXCITING TITLES
By Michael Scantlebury

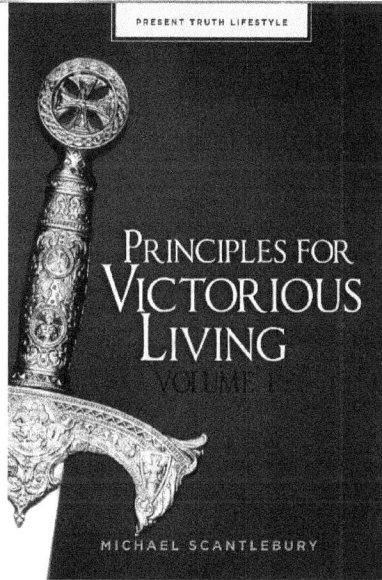

Principles For Victorious Living Volume I

The information contained herein is well balanced with a spiritual maturity that keenly stems from wisdom and revelation in the knowledge of Christ. This is the anointing of an Apostle, and the truths that our brother shares will certainly cause you to excel in the Kingdom of God long before this life is over when later we enter the eternals. There's so much to experience today in this life, and Michael extracts so much from the Word of God to facilitate that. His insight of revelation and ability to interpret and articulate what his spirit receives from the Lord are powerful.

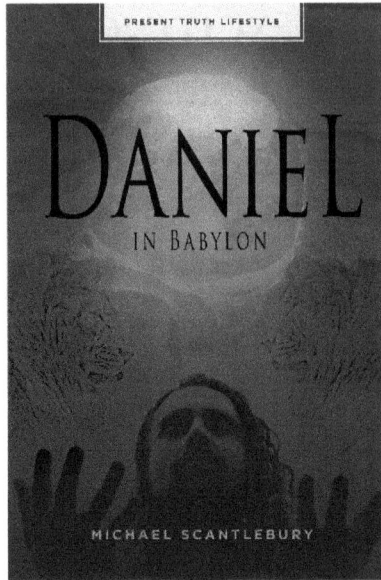

Present Truth Lifestyle – Daniel In Babylon

This is a seminal study with strong Apostolic messaging, yet its flowing style allows for easy assimilation of biblical truths, and provides accurate insights for the cerebral believer, who like Daniel and his companions, are usually the target of the world system. In this book various methodologies are outlined through which, spiritual Babylon seeks to entice the brightest and best of every Godly generation, to acculturize, rob of spiritual identity and manipulate to promote world kingdom end.

But thanks be to God, there is still a generation in the earth spiritually alert enough to operate within the world system, yet deploy their talents and giftings to bring honour and glory to God. Those with the Daniel mindset will decode dreams and visions and interpret judgements written on the kingdoms of this world in this season.

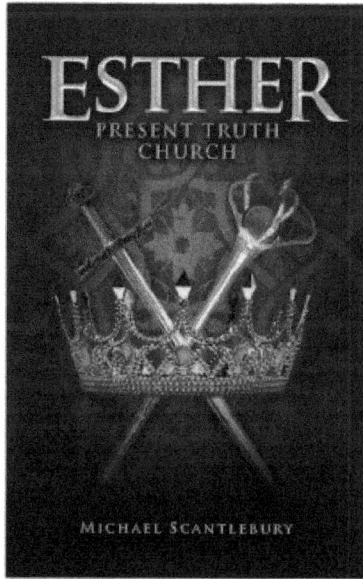

Esther Present Truth Church

In a season where the Church co-exists harmoniously with truth and error, this book provides us with a precision tool and well-calibrated instrument of change that is able to fine-tune the global Body of Christ.

The Book of Esther is rich with revelation that is still valid and applicable for the day in which we live. Hidden within its pages is a powerful "present truth" message. The lives of the people involved and the conditions that are seen have spiritual parallels for the Church. Our destiny as the Body of Christ is revealed. The preparations and conditions we must attain to are all similar.

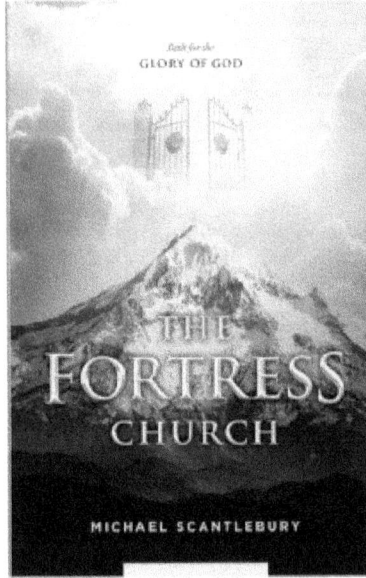

The Fortress Church

According to Webster's English Dictionary "fortress" is defined as: a fortified place: stronghold, *especially*: A large and permanent fortification sometimes including a town. A place that is protected against attack. This book seeks to describe what is a "Fortress Church". We would be looking into the dynamics of this Church as described in Jacob's vision in Genesis Chapter 28, also as described by the Prophet Isaiah, in Isaiah Chapter 2 and as the one detailed in a Psalm of the sons of Korah in Psalms Chapter 48. We would also be looking at a working model of this type of church as found at Antioch in the Book of Acts. Finally we would be exploring The Church at Ephesus, where the Apostle Paul by the Holy Spirit revealed some powerful descriptions of The Church.

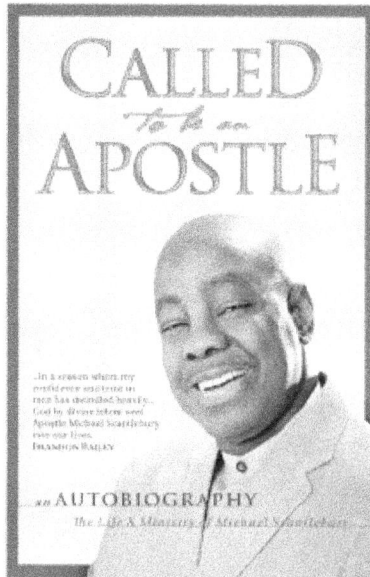

Called To Be An Apostle

This autobiography spans fifty-two years of my life on the earth thus far and I have the hope of living several more... Our home was always packed with young people and we did enjoy times of really wonderful fellowship! Although we were experiencing these wonderful times of fellowship my appetite and desire to grow in the things of God continued unabated. I continued to read anything and everything that I could put my hands on that would strengthen my life. I began reading Wigglesworth, Moody, Finney, Idahosa, Lake, and the list went on and on! But the more I read the more this question burned in my heart—"why is it that every time we hear/read about a move of God, it is always miles away and in another country? Why can't I experience some of the things that I am reading about?" Little did I know the Lord would answer that desire!

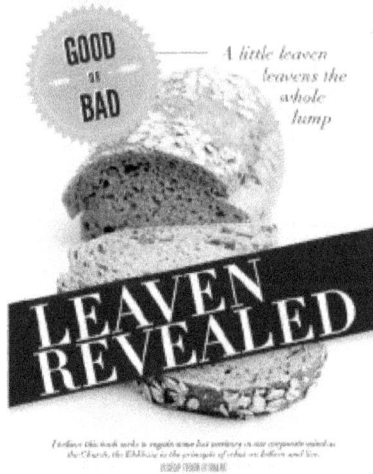

Leavened Revealed

The Bible has a lot to say about *leaven* and its effects upon the Believer. Leaven as an ingredient gives a false sense of growth. In the New Testament there are at least six types of *leaven* spoken about and we will be exploring them in detail, in order to ensure that our lives are completely free of the first five, and completely influenced by the sixth! These types of leaven include the following: The leaven of the Pharisees; The leaven of the Sadducees; The leaven of the Galatians; The leaven of Herod; The leaven of the Corinthians. However, the Leaven of the Kingdom of God is the only type of leaven that has the power and capacity to bring about true growth and lasting change to our lives.

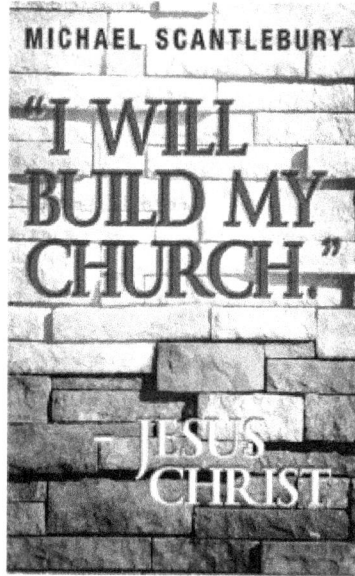

I Will Build My Church – Jesus Christ

"For we are his *masterpiece*, created in Christ Jesus for good works that God prepared long ago to be our way of life." Ephesians 2:10

What a powerful picture of The Church of Jesus Christ—-His Masterpiece! Reference to a *masterpiece* lends to the idea that there are other pieces and among them all, this particular one stands head and shoulders above the rest! This is so true when it comes to The Church that Jesus Christ is building; when you place it alongside everything else that God has created, The Church is by far His Masterpiece!

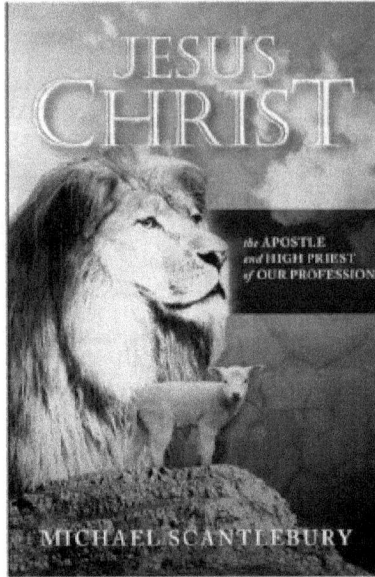

Jesus Christ The Apostle And High Priest Of Our Profession

There is a dimension to the apostolic nature of Jesus Christ that I would like to capture in His one-on-one encounters with several people during the time He walked the face of the earth and functioned as Apostle. In this book we will explore several significant encounters that Jesus Christ had with different people where valuable principles and insight can be gleaned. They are designed to change your life.

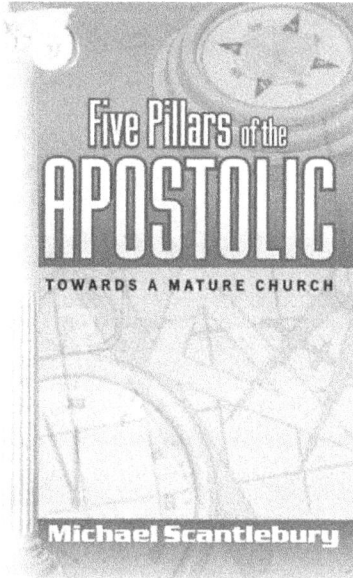

Five Pillars Of The Apostolic

It has become very evident that a new day has dawned in the earth, as the Lord restores the foundational ministry of the Apostle back to His Church. This book will give you a clear and concise understanding of what the Holy Spirit is doing in The Church today.

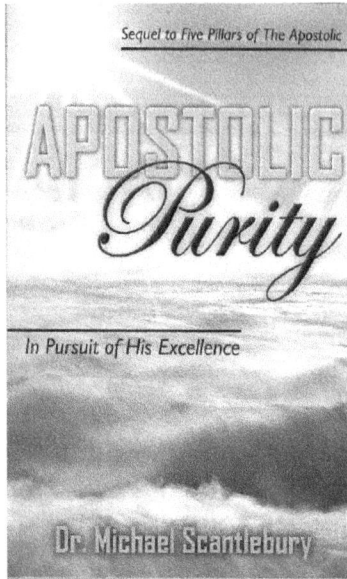

Apostolic Purity

In every dispensation, in every move of God's Holy Spirit to bring restoration and reformation to His Church, righteousness, holiness and purity has always been of utmost importance to the Lord. This book will challenge your to walk pure as you seek to fulfil God's Will for your life and ministry.

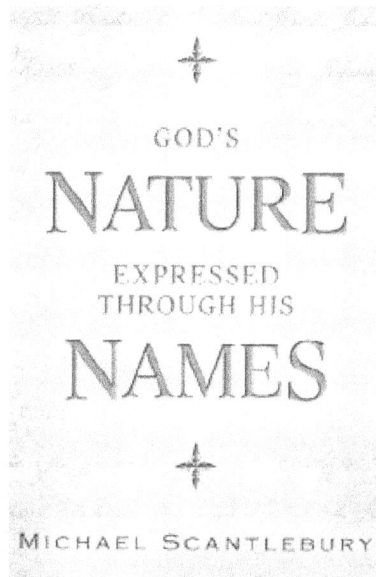

God's Nature Expressed Through His Names

How awesome it would be when we encounter God's Nature through the varied expressions of His Names. His Names give us reference and guidance as to how He works towards and in us as His people—and by extension to society! As a matter of fact it adds a whole new meaning to how you draw near to Him; and by this you can now begin to know His Ways because you have come into relationship with His Nature.

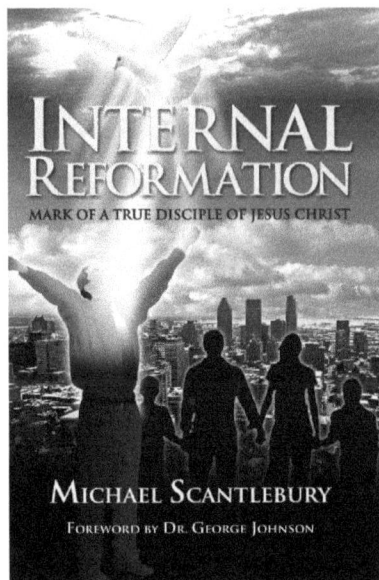

Internal Reformation

Internal Reformation is multifaceted. It is an ecclesiology laying out the blue print of The Church Jesus Christ is building in today's world. At the same time it is a manual laying out the modus operandi of how Believers are called to function as dynamic, militant over-comers who are powerful because they carry internally the very character and DNA of Jesus Christ.

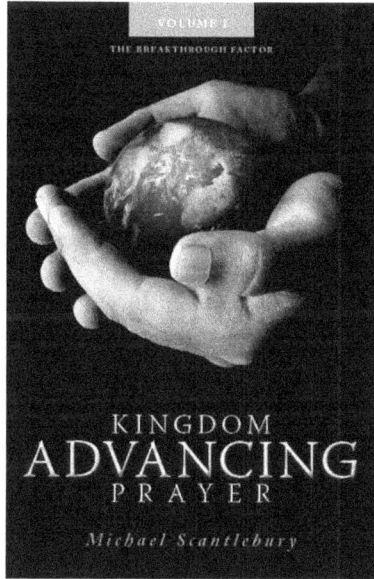

Kingdom Advancing Prayer Volume I

The Church of Jesus Christ is stronger and much more determined and equipped than she has ever been, and strong, aggressive, powerful, Spirit-Filled, Kingdom-centred prayers are being lifted in every nation in the earth. This kind of prayer is released from the heart of Father God into the hearts of His people, as we seek for His Glory to cover the earth as the waters cover the sea.

Apostolic Reformation

If the axe is dull, And one does not sharpen the edge, Then he must use more strength; But wisdom brings success." (Ecclesiastes 10:10) For centuries The Church of Jesus Christ has been using quite a bit of strength while working with a dull axe (sword, Word of God, revelation), in trying to get the job done. This has been largely due to the fact that she has been functioning without Apostles, the ones who have been graced and anointed by the Lord, with the ability to sharpen.

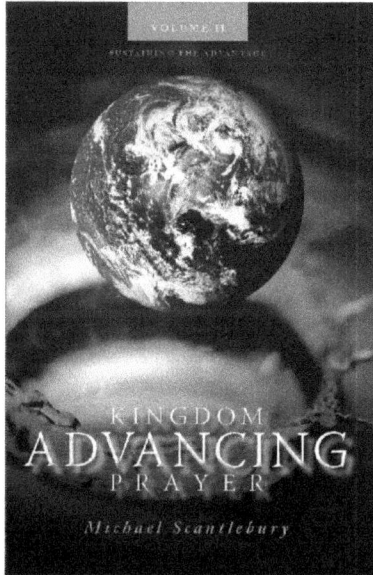

Kingdom Advancing Prayer Volume II

Prayer is calling for the Bridegroom's return, and for the Bride to be made ready. Prayers are storming the heavens and binding the "strong men" declaring and decreeing God's Kingdom rule in every jurisdiction. This is what we call Kingdom Advancing Prayer. What a *Glorious Day* to be *Alive* and to be in the *Will* and *Plan of Father God*! *Hallelujah*!

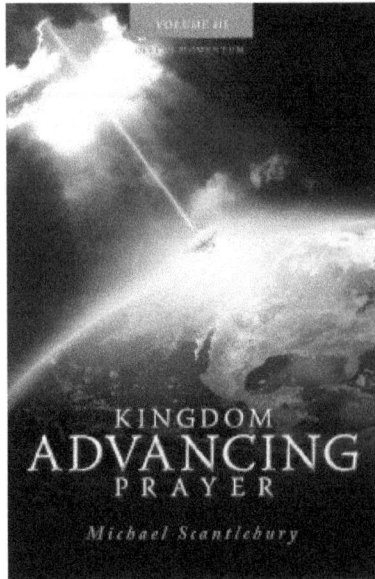

Kingdom Advancing Prayer Volume III

One of the keys to the amazing rise to greater functionality of The Church is the clear understanding of what we call Kingdom Advancing Prayer. This kind of prayer reaches into the very core of the demonic stronghold and destroys demonic kings and princes and establishes the Kingdom and Purpose of the Lord. This is the kind of prayer that Jesus Christ engaged in, to bring to pass the will of His Father while He was upon planet earth.

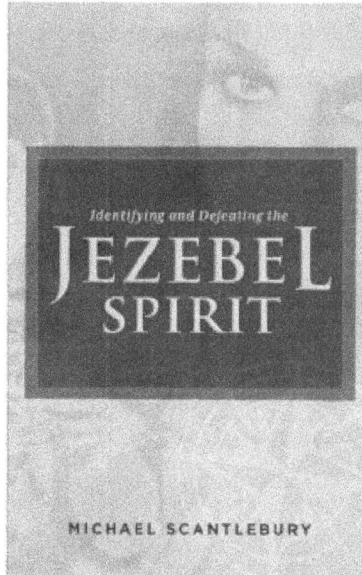

Identifying And Defeating The Jezebel Spirit

I declare to you with the greatest of conviction that we are living in the days when Malachi 4:5-6 is being fulfilled. Elijah in his day had to confront and deal with a false spiritual order and government that was established and set up by an evil woman called Jezebel and her spineless husband called Ahab. This spirit is still active in the earth and in The Church; however the Lord is restoring His holy Apostles and Prophets to identify and destroy this spirit as recorded in Revelation 2:18-23.

Ordering Information

Book Orders Please Contact:
Word Alive Press

In Canada | USA:
Phone: 866.967.3782 | Fax: 800.352.9272
International: Phone: 204.667.1400 | Fax: 204.669.0947
Website – www.wordalive.ca

Or From:
Present Truth Media

Phone: 604.599.3542 | Fax: 604.599.3543
Website – https://present-truthpublishing.com

Also Available From:
www.amazon.ca/com
www.chapters.Indigo.ca
www.barnesandnoble.com

www.ingramcontent.com/pod-product-compliance
Lightning Source LLC
Chambersburg PA
CBHW061725020426
42331CB00006B/1102